"Who's afraid of birthdays?
One, two, three, four, five—I could
hardly wait for ten. Thirteen, fourteen,
fifteen—I could hardly wait for twenty.
Graduations, marriage and three babies
(one at a time!)—and I was satisfied with forty.
The birthdays kept on coming! Fifty wasn't so bad.
I could scarcely believe sixty. Then retirement
into a whole new life at sixty-five. Another ten years
have gone and the next birthday is seventy-six.
I really can't believe it. Life is more exciting
and fulfilling than ever. *So* birthdays
don't count. *It is life that counts.*"

—from the Preface

So Who's Afraid of Birthdays

Anna B. Mow

TRUMPET BOOKS
Published by
A. J. HOLMAN COMPANY
division of J. B. LIPPINCOTT COMPANY
PHILADELPHIA and NEW YORK

Published by Pillar Books for A. J. Holman Company

Copyright © 1969 by Anna B. Mow

Printed in the United States of America

ISBN: 0-87981-054-8

The quotations from *The New Testament in Modern English* translated by J. B. Phillips are reprinted with permission of The Macmillan Company, copyright © 1958 by J. B. Phillips.

Where not otherwise indicated, Biblical citations are taken from the Revised Standard Version of the Holy Bible. Copyright 1946 and 1952 by the Division of Christian Education of the National Council of the Churches of Christ in the United States of America. Used by permission.

"The Look Ahead" is from a volume of poems by Edwin Markham entitled *Eighty Songs at Eighty* published by Doubleday and Company in 1932. Reprinted by permission of Virgil Markham.

Dedicated to My Father,
I. N. H. Beahm,
Who Was Still Young at Ninety-one

Contents

Preface

Who's afraid of birthdays? One, two, three, four, five—I could hardly wait for ten. Thirteen, fourteen, fifteen—I could hardly wait for twenty. Graduations, marriage, and three babies (one at a time!)—and I was satisfied with forty. The birthdays kept coming! Fifty wasn't so bad. I could scarcely believe sixty. Then retirement into a whole new life at sixty-five. Another ten years have gone and the next birthday is seventy-five. I really can't believe it. Life is more exciting and fulfilling than ever. *So* birthdays don't count. It is *life* that counts.

Whenever I think of life, or real zest for living, I think of my father. He never grew old, so I have dedicated this book to him. We have a home now because he bought a house at ninety-one! A neighbor told me that the day after my father moved here he called in all the neighbor children and entertained them with many stories. His second night here was his last, for he was killed in an automobile accident on a preaching tour.

My father was loved by young and old alike. Legends about him have grown through the years. He always spoke of himself in the third person:

"Brother Beahm is here!" I haven't always thought so, but perhaps he really was objective about himself. Two great railroads favored him by stopping any train for him in our small village south of Washington, D.C. I'm sure he had the same favor at the heavenly gate. Our pastor's announcement of his death read: "Last night at eleven o'clock the Angel Gabriel looked down the streets of heaven and said, 'Why look, Brother Beahm is here!' " He must have been as welcome there as he was in a thousand homes on earth.

No matter what happened—and his life was not easy—he never lost courage, a courage made of endurance and hope. Anyone who never loses courage or hope is free to look for the best in the future. So many of us have no expectancy. A little old lady came to talk to me after I spoke at a meeting one night. "How are you?" I asked. She replied in a despairing tone, "Pretty good for my age." I asked her age. She was ten years younger than I! It is *expecting* aches, pains, and disabilities that is so devastating. Browning knew better:

> Grow old along with me!
> The best is yet to be, . . .

We can turn the old adage around, "As long as there is hope there is life." Birthdays *don't* count, and we need not fear to count them. I'll be seventy-six or more by the time you read my book, which is my simple effort to prove to you that we need *not* be afraid of birthdays.

It is more than a form for me to express appreciation to my husband, Baxter, in this book, for he has been my star witness of a happy retired man. Eugenia Price and my editor keep me out of ruts and meaningless alleys. And what would I do without Cecile Dowdy who does the typing and is ever ready for any counsel I might need?

Thanks to all the nice older people who let me share their stories with you.

ANNA B. MOW

Roanoke, Virginia

So Who's Afraid of Birthdays

Chapter 1

Are You Flexible?

My host in an Ohio home recently told me about his mother who lives in the southern mountains. She cannot even remember when she started to use snuff. Not long ago, at the age of ninety, she announced to her family at the dinner table, "It has just dawned on me that using snuff is a dirty habit. I'm stopping right now!" And she did.

If you think this woman is rigid and provincial because she has lived in one secluded area all her life, you are mistaken. She keeps her eye on what's coming up and not on what's slipping by. She's *flexible,* not rigid. She lives with an air of expectancy, ready for any surprises life may bring.

The Associated Press carried a similar story from Bristol, England. A Mr. Charlie Brown at ninety-seven married eighty-two-year-old Annie Wintle. He announced to reporters, "I got tired of the single life and I'm giving up beer, Annie doesn't like it." Old Charlie is young enough even to change his habits for love of another. That is not only flexibility for change but flexibility for relationship.

One of the most colorful young "old ladies" I ever met was in a village in India. I went to her home to meet the daughter, a junior in a Bombay college, who was home on vacation. This was at the height of Gandhi's freedom movement, so, of course,

I asked the girl what she thought of the new freedom coming to the women of India. She started to answer, then interrupted herself; "You should talk to my mother, she has wonderful ideas." She called her mother, and a tiny old wrinkled woman came trotting alertly in. Not only her mind, but all her muscles were flexible! The daughter listened with great respect as her mother expressed her views. Not only had this woman always lived in one village, she had never been to school a day in her life. Lack of formal education had not limited her mind's capacity to develop new ideas.

And she was not illiterate. She had her first child teach her to read as he learned to read during his first year in school. The desire for education came to her when, as a very young bride, she first heard Mahatma Gandhi speak. He opened a window in her mind to the outside world. In spite of the fears of her caste family, she saw to it that her children were educated. As we talked together, her son was on his way home from England with a Ph.D.

Each one of these "old people" still had the ability to change. Each one showed the adventure of youth stabilized by a wise purpose in life. Each was flexible enough for steady growth and change.

In fact, there is no growth of any kind without the ability and willingness to change. Do you remember how you wanted to change when you were young, how you wanted to grow up? And how important it was each year to be promoted to the next grade in school? You need not look back with longing, you can keep that same youthful spirit which is always on the alert to investigate more of life. You can find real delight in developing your own inner resources, as well as the resources of a new or a familiar environment.

True maturity is the ability to change in order to reach a desired goal. The goal provides the stability that keeps one from seeking security in the inertia of the same old ways in order to avoid the pressures of circumstances that may change rapidly. It has been said that old age begins the moment we lose this flexibility for change.

Those without a goal may merely yield to a changing environment and mistakenly think that they are growing. The apostle Paul says to them, "Don't let the world around you squeeze you into its own mold, but let God remold your minds from within, so that you may prove in practice that the plan of God for you is good, meets all His demands and moves toward the goal of true maturity" (Romans 12:2, Phillips).

This inner stability prepares one for the shocks that come from crises over which we have no control. Even birthdays become crises for some people. But birthdays come no matter how we feel about them. *How we feel about them* is ours to decide, and the person who does not fight change can look forward to each added year. Each year holds its joys and compensations for the one who welcomes growing change. To a person who has learned to welcome growth, a birthday is never a crisis. It is a joyous celebration.

For the one who has never lost the ability to handle change, mandatory retirement at sixty-five or seventy will never be a tragedy. The adventure of

living does not end with the conclusion of a job or
a profession. If you are open you are set for new
joys and wonders ahead. If this is your experience
you will understand the words Robert Browning
spoke through Rabbi Ben Ezra:

> *Grow old along with me!*
> *The best is yet to be,*
> *The last of life, for which the first was made; .*
> *Our times are in His hand*
> *Who saith, "A whole I planned,*
> *Youth shows but half; Trust God, see all, nor be*
> *afraid!"*

. . . .

> *Therefore I summon age*
> *To grant youth's heritage . . .*
> *Youth ended, I shall try*
> *My gain or loss thereby;*
> *Leave the fire ashes, what survives is gold. . . .*

Chapter 2

Are You Ready for the Best?

"The best is yet to be" if one has been growing all the time. But some people are not ready for this *best*. Are you one of them?

Many of us hold back because we are afraid of being too changeable. We are afraid that flexibility is the same as vacillation. We see such irresponsibility in others and harden ourselves against being too easygoing.

There is reason for this fear, but one need not be bound by it. It is the *goal* that makes the difference. The person who really vacillates is *circumstance*-conditioned and has no point of reference for his reactions to whatever happens to him. The maturely flexible person is really moving forward in the turmoil of outer changes because his reactions are determined by the inner pattern or goal of his life.

Real problems are ahead for those who have lost their ability to change, who have settled down too much in a certain way of living, with the same neighbors, the same uniformity in their own church group, the same accepted prejudices (which they call "convictions"), the same religious words used about religious living, the same version of the Bible, the same everything. Everything is static. Somewhere along the line growth stopped. Then life brings changes that are beyond their control; they are rigid and brittle—and they break.

There are too many good people in this category. They mean well, but the older they get the more rigid and hard they become. They seem to have *rigor mortis* on the inside while their physical bodies live on. I remember one such man who seemed dead inside twenty years before his body was ready for burial. He was an emotional burden to his family, to his church, and to his community. It must have been a relief to bury him.

If you know people like this, do not give up on them. There is always hope, if you are really concerned. Israel was in such a condition and the prophet told them a delightful graveyard story! (See Ezekiel 37:1–14.)

The hand of the Lord was upon me, and he brought me out by the Spirit of the Lord, and set me down in the midst of the valley; it was full of bones. And he led me round among them; and behold, there were very many upon the valley; and lo, *they were very dry*. And he said to me, "Son of man, can these bones live?" And I answered, "O Lord God, thou knowest." Again he said to me, "Prophesy to these bones, and say to them, O dry bones, hear the word of the Lord. Thus says the Lord God to these bones: Behold, I will cause breath to enter you, and you shall live. And I will lay sinews upon you, and will cause flesh to come upon you, and cover you

with skin, and put breath in you, and you shall
live; and you shall know that I am the Lord."

Ezekiel prophesied as he was commanded and the
bones came together into bodies, but there was no
breath in them. Ezekiel prophesied again and
"breath came into them, and they lived, and stood
upon their feet, an exceedingly great host."

If you will overlook the gruesome picture in this
parable you will get a peep at the humor of God,
which is really *hope*. This parable was a message for
the people who had given up hope for their country
and for God's interest in them. We have the same
Lord God, but we know even more about Him because of Jesus Christ. So we have even greater reason for hope when He promises, "I will put my
Spirit within you, and *you shall live*."

To live and keep on living there must be continuous change. This change comes in the process of
renewal. This is true physically. The healthy body
is being constantly renewed. This is also just as true
mentally and spiritually. There is so much in God's
Word about renewal of life that it is strange that
any conscientious Christian would be afraid of
change in his outlook on life or even in his religious ideas. Of course, the fear is that change would
mean loss of faith, but this is never true if the faith
is in the living God and not in one's ideas of God.
God never changes, but our minds must be open to
new knowledge or grow stagnant. When we quit
growing we begin to die. Renewal can come to anyone at any time by turning to God in faith.

The church at Sardis was pronounced dead but

called to new life: "I know your works; you have the name of being alive, and you are dead. Awake, and strengthen what remains and is on the point of death, for I have not found your works perfect in the sight of my God "(Revelation 3:1–2).

Saul, the Pharisee, was one of the most inflexible religious men of any day. He was thoroughly convinced that it was heresy to believe in Jesus as the Messiah. He was conscientious, honest, and completely committed to God's Word. So when he met Jesus as living Lord on the Damascus road, his honesty and dedication to God made it possible for him to change at once when he saw that *Jesus* was God's Word. He could even change the content of his faith when God showed him where he was wrong. So now we know this man not as rigid Saul but as Paul, the free apostle. (Read Acts 9:1–9 and Philippians 3:1–11.)

This was for Paul only the beginning of many changes because he was now set for growth. He said, "And we all, with unveiled face, beholding the glory of the Lord, are being changed into his likeness from one degree of glory to another . . ." (2 Corinthians 3:18).

To the Philippian church, Paul wrote about the same need for growth, "Not that I have already obtained this or am already perfect; but I press on to make it my own, because Christ Jesus has made me his own. Brethren, I do not consider that I have made it my own; but one thing I do, forgetting what lies behind and straining forward to what lies ahead, I press on toward the goal for the prize of the upward call of God in Christ Jesus" (Philippians 3:12–14).

If we do not learn to keep on growing there will soon be too many half-dead people walking around. In 1900 only one in every twenty-five persons in our total population was over sixty-five. By 1950 the ratio was one in twelve. According to the Bureau of Census estimates, by 1975 nearly twenty-two million persons will be sixty-five and over compared to a little over twelve million in 1950. We don't want to be a dead weight on our loved ones or on our country. We must find our own way to continued growth and vital interest in life.

God wants, with all His longing heart, to give us His best. Can you think of anything that might make your later years more livable than to know you have God's best for them? The best is yet to come for us all, if we are ready for it. To be ready means to set a goal and keep it (at my age) and press on, as Paul suggests, toward that goal—our ears tuned to God's harmony, and our minds and spirits flexible enough to enter into that harmony. Even God's harmony can be thrown off when one man or woman insists upon doing the conducting.

We are ready for God's best when we are open to receive it. His best is always ready for us—ready and waiting.

Chapter 3

Do You Have Security?

I read not long ago that young men applying for their first jobs were more concerned about retirement benefits than about the job. So much is said about "old age" these days that even the young are afraid of it. Planning a life colored by this fear is completely different from *living* it in such a way that one knows "the best is yet to be." To many of us *security* means "social security" plus all the accrued benefits from a lifetime of service. But economic security is not enough to make the "last of life" the kind "for which the first was made."

There are years between the first and the last of life. Many join the "rat race" and attempt to keep up with the latest in everything and wonder why a desired sense of security eludes them.

Others live along day by day taking what life brings until sudden changes shake them. This is true of many older people today. In rural America there was seldom great change with advancing age. People did not retire then. They just went on in their same way of living and working until they could go no longer. Parents took less and less responsibility as the years passed and children took more. Perhaps the "old folks" merely moved to a downstairs bedroom in one wing of the big house. They usually found plenty to do without getting in anyone's way.

Those "good old days" are gone forever. Houses are smaller, too small for two generations—to say nothing of three—under the same roof.

At mandatory retirement age many men and woman are still in their prime. Indeed some specialists are saying that *the prime of life for a growing person is not reached until seventy-five.* For the person whose security is in his career, "retirement" can be a devastating experience. If one's home must also be changed the sense of security is even more shaken. One man who had refused to face the inevitable change exclaimed, "I wish they'd line me up and shoot me!"

People resent retirement because it emphasizes advancing age for which they have not prepared themselves. But age advances anyway, whether one has sense enough to prepare for it or not. So why not make it a real advancement?

Edwin Markham knew the secret:

I am done with the years that were: I am quits:
  I am done with the dead and the old.
They are mines worked out: I delved in their pits:
  I have saved their grain of gold.

Now I turn to the future for wine and bread:
  I have bidden the past adieu,
I laugh and lift hand to the years ahead:
  *"Come on: I am ready for you!"**

Retirement? No! Adventure? Yes! But in any case it is hard to quit when one has been active for

---

* From "The Look Ahead."

many years. It's the quitting that is hard. It's the loss of familiar possessions in the "quitting" that makes it hard and often prolongs the agony. It takes a real sense of values to make such a transition. Some months ago we had dinner in a lovely home with friends who were facing the disposal of many of their belongings which they could not take with them to the three rooms of their new apartment. Of course, their possessions that stood for memories of family living, of anniversaries, of travels were more than mere "things." They symbolized sixty years of memories together. The children were all married and scattered. To each was given what would have been inherited later anyway. Disposal of the loved grand piano to strangers brought the heartache; no one had room for it.

With courage the disposal was made and they were "quits" with the past. They are now happy in their three rooms with a view of the mountains and no cares or responsibilities beyond their small place. They are free to do the traveling they enjoy, and they also found a new freedom in the discovery that they were not possessed by their "things."

This was not true of a rich widow in Chicago. Her only security was in her things. "YOU CAN'T TAKE IT WITH YOU" was the headline for the startling story about her in the newspaper. The ninety-four-year-old widow had died, and few seemed to know anything about her. The Chicago Title and Trust Co. was named conservator of her estate, which after inventory was valued at a half-million dollars. In 1885 this woman had moved into a new mansion at 1500 West Jackson, and there she spent the rest of her life. After the loss of her immediate family she turned to *things* until they possessed her. For fifty-three years she collected beautiful antiques. She filled her three-story house until she had only one room left for living, on the third floor. It contained a brass bed, two chairs, a marble-topped bureau, and a piano. Then she bought other properties, thirty in all, to contain her treasures. One of these was a twenty-room mansion which she purchased for thirty-two thousand dollars. Her love for beautiful things became a fever—but strangers made the inventory of the fifteen thousand items which she could not take with her out of this world.

Things become too important when they become a substitute for the security one has not found in relationships. And the relationship which puts everything into focus is the priceless relationship we may each have with the living God who is our Heavenly Father. Jesus said that if we seek God first all other things will take their proper place (Matthew 6:33).

Of course, there are many who have faced subtraction rather than addition of things when they put God first. We marvel at their joy in God and at their lack of a sense of loss in things.

Pervin was a young Parsi girl who lived next door to us in India when our children were small. They were great friends and she always enjoyed story hours with them, especially the stories of Jesus. Eventually Pervin wanted to become a Christian. Her father considered himself a very liberal Parsi, but he was not liberal enough to permit his daughter to follow Christ. He believed that one could be a Parsi only by birth and that no one born a Parsi could be "un-Parsied."

After we left India, Pervin could not forget Christ, so she took the only course open to her. She became a Christian, left home, accepted disinheritance and separation from her family. Later she married a Christian young man whom she had met at our house—a teacher on a small salary. After fifteen years he died suddenly, and left Pervin with less than three dollars and a partially blind son. Her troubles were increased by her own ill health.

When after twenty-five years we returned to India we made a special point of visiting Pervin. She had been reluctant to write us about her needs because she was afraid we would worry about her. Even though she calls me "mother," it was not easy to discover how really poor she had been. She was more interested in talking about what Christ means to her then in discussing her poverty.

Knowing the lovely home she had once lived in, I finally learned that she now lived in a windowless, ten-foot-square room that had been a horse stable. Still she was as immaculately clean as ever and she walked with the same queenly dignity.

After her husband died, the Parsis crowded around her, declaring, "Your Christian husband is dead. Now you can be a Parsi again." She answered, "I am a Christian because I love the Lord Jesus Christ."

To me she said, "Jesus was born in a stable and I can live in one for Him. Never feel sorry for me. I am richer than many people who live in mansions." She is in her late fifties now—not strong in body, but growing stronger in faith. Being with Pervin gives one a renewed sense of *security in God,* a security that cannot be shaken by anything that can happen in this life.

Anyone who who makes the choice of security in God rather than earthly security is entering into the fellowship of the apostle Paul. He could not have both securities, either. He knew the security of family, prestige, honor, education, but this security he let go when he became a follower of Christ. He said, "But whatever gain I had, I counted as loss for the sake of Christ. Indeed I count everything as loss because of the surpassing worth of knowing Christ Jesus my Lord. For his sake I have suffered the loss of all things, and count them as refuse, in order that I may gain Christ" (Philippians 3:7–8).

To the Corinthian church, Paul wrote: "This priceless treasure we hold, so to speak, in a common earthenware jar—to show that the splendid power of it belongs to God and not to us. We are handicapped on all sides, but we are never frustrated; we are puzzled, but never in despair. We are persecuted, but we never have to stand it alone: we may be knocked down but we are never knocked out!" (2 Corinthians 4:7–9, Phillips).

This is the lasting, unshakable security—not in things, but in a constant relationship with the living God. Don't expect it from any other source. It won't be there. This does not mean we will have no need of enough money—we all share that need. What it means is that in the security found in God is enough to supply *all needs—spiritual, physical, material.* In fact, Jesus promised, "Seek first his kingdom and his righteousness, and all these things shall be yours as well" (Matthew 6:33).

Chapter 4

Is Your Religion Life or Rites?

There were two sisters: One was the widow of a minister, and certain that she was the "religious" one. She read her Bible every day, spent a specific time in prayer, never missed a church service—still people would cross the street to avoid passing her, because her tongue was so sharp. Her religion was all in performing certain acts. The other sister made no show of her religion, but just being in her presence made everyone God-conscious. She loved and welcomed everyone she encountered.

The first sister made people feel dead, the second one made everyone feel alive. She *was* alive in God.

To people like the first sister Jesus said, "Not every one who says to me, 'Lord, Lord,' shall enter the kingdom of heaven" (Matthew 7:21). (Such people would be miserable in heaven!) Religious words, religious forms and disciplines, even the right ones, are not enough. A relationship with God is the essential factor.

It is possible to know about God and not know *Him* at all. Our attitude toward those who think of God in a different way from ours may reveal the true story of our own condition.

It is so easy when we talk about God to think

that our own way of thinking is the only right way and everyone else is on the wrong path.

Or as we meet other Christians with different interpretations we may become protective of our own and think we are defending the faith when we are merely defending our own opinions. (The fact is, faith does not need defending, it only needs proclaiming!)

Also, when we become argumentative we are inclined to put all our beliefs in a package. Then we are afraid to consider even one of our points as untenable for fear we will lose our whole bundle of faith. This might even be because we carried the package of our beliefs whole from childhood days and never learned to distinguish form from reality.

If this has happened to you, you have missed one of the great experiences of adolescence, the time when you began to wonder about the faith of your childhood. Perhaps some loved one said your wondering was sinful doubt. Too bad! That was the time to think through what you had accepted with the credulity of childhood and to make it yours through *your own thinking*. Honest doubt is never sin, it is the reasoning faculty God gave us to serve our faith. If you missed this experience thirty years ago, it is not too late. Do it now.

Too often we forget that God expects us to use the minds He gave us. A university woman once said to me, "My religion is not for my mind, it is for my feelings. I use my mind in my academic work and that has nothing to do with my religion." I was surprised to find a university woman so uneducated about religion.

We can think *about* God, even to changing many ideas about Him and at the same time be growing in our relationship with Him. Indeed, if our ideas about God do not grow (that means change), I doubt if we can maintain real relationship with Him. This may be the reason many people have a dried-up religion rather than a living faith. The outstanding characteristic about Christianity is that we can have relationship with a living God, and our faith is in Him even more than in our ideas about Him.

Geography may be a conditioning factor also. Did you ever stop to consider how many of your ideas and "convictions" may be yours only because you have lived in the same area all your life? It is good to have our beliefs tested for relative merit by contact with other people whom we respect and who may have different views. This kind of exposure often does not happen until people retire, and then they are not always flexible enough to act in a mature Christian way.

It is interesting to see what occurs when people from different parts of the country move to southern California or Florida. Some are so set in their own ideas that they have no undersanding left for anyone who does not agree with them. They are a disruptive force wherever they go.

How could good people who have always been conscientious get into such a state of hardness? The symbols of their faith and doctrine somewhere along the line must have become an end in themselves. Then their security gradually rested in the outer observance of the symbols rather than in the Reality that the symbols represented.

The symbols are fine and we cannot discard them, but neither can we find real security in them alone. When they become an end in themselves they become *things* in religion. By another name this is idolatry.

Happily, not everyone has this difficulty. There are many who still have enough of the love of God in their hearts to be able to listen to others, even if they still agree to differ. A continuous relationship with God who is Love, who is Reality is the only assurance anyone can have that He still is at the center of truth.

There has always been the danger of substituting form for Reality. This is what Paul meant when he wrote to the Corinthians, "The written code kills, but the Spirit gives life" (2 Corinthians 3:6). This is an astounding statement because Paul was talking about Scripture!

The Scriptures are symbols, too, of God's holy, living Word. Jesus warned the Pharisees, specialists in the use of the Scriptures, against their *misuse*. He said to them, "You search the scriptures, because you think that in them you have eternal life; and it is they that bear witness to me; yet you refuse to come to me that you may have life" (John 5:39–40). Even the Scriptures cannot be an end in themselves, Jesus said—this is Bibliolatry. The Scriptures are given to us to reveal Jesus Christ and to reveal God through Him.

How subtle the spiritual perversion can become if the emphasis is put in the wrong place! The priests who were the leaders in the temple worship and who were particular about ceremonial cleanliness were the very ones who led in the trial against Jesus. "They themselves did not enter the praetorium, so that *they might not be defiled, but might eat the passover*" (John 18:28). They knew only the symbols, the *things* of worship, and did not understand what real spiritual defilement was because they apparently had no real life in God.

Even the early Christians had the same tendency to hold onto the symbol while they forgot its meaning. Paul had to tell the Corinthian church: "I do not commend you, because when you come together it is not for the better but for the worse" (1 Corinthians 11:17). Just meeting in the church service was not enough. They even took communion and missed its real value. They did not discern the meaning of the symbol and thereby condemned themselves (1 Corinthians 11:29–30). The tendency is always to "holding the form of religion but denying the power of it" (2 Timothy 3:5).

The only assurance we can have that we are growing *toward* more of life and that we are not slipping into dead ways is through a living relationship with a living Lord through the power of the Holy Spirit. Through the Spirit, discernment grows so that we can know which way we are going.

If you know people who are too legalistic, remember they may seem hard because of fear. Many are afraid to change religious habits or ideas lest they lose what reality they do have. This is why the most conscientious people sometimes get caught on this dead-end street. Do not attack their fears, but underscore their faith in God. Remember, "The Lord is faithful; he will strengthen you and guard you from evil" (2 Thessalonians 3:3).

With eyes wide open to the mercies of God, I beg you, my brothers, as an act of intelligent worship, to give him your bodies, as a living sacrifice, consecrated to him and acceptable by him. Don't let the world around you squeeze you into its own mold, but let God remold your minds from within, so that you may prove in practice that the plan of God for you is good, meets all his demands and moves toward the goal of true maturity.

Romans 12:1–2, Phillips

Such is the confidence that we have through Christ toward God . . . for the written code kills, but the Spirit gives life.

2 Corinthians 3:4,6

Chapter 5

How Do You View the Church?

In the 1930s Hitler said, "One more push and the church will be gone." Now some leaders inside the church are saying almost the same thing. Good people are bewildered. I am often asked, "What do you think of the church?" I always ask, "Which church do you mean? The institutional church or the Church which is the Body of Christ?"

Changes in the institutional church do not bother me, but the Church which is the Body of Christ is impregnable, "and the powers of death shall not prevail against it" (Matthew 16:18). If we keep these two phases of the church in mind we will not be confused.

Some people cannot stand changes even in the building in which the church meets. I was in a church once which was in the process of building new Sunday school rooms. The oldest brother in the congregation was very much opposed to the building program. He said, "This old building was good enough for me all my life, it is good enough for my grandchildren." I was invited to this man's home for dinner before an evening communion service. I expected an old farmhouse with no modern improvements. But no! They had every modern convenience, even luxuries. As I left the elderly brother said, "I'll be a little late for communion. I have to see my program on television before I come!" The angels smiled—*and* shed a tear for the old man's blindness.

All of us who are of this generation of "retired people" remember back to our teens when the church was the social center of each community. The yearly revival meetings were the main social event of the community. The "in group" was the church group, the rest were "sinners" who became the center of attention at a revival. It was the church people who labeled outsiders "sinners."

Times have changed. There are many rivals for the attention of the people in all communities. When the church is little more than a religious club, why should anyone want to come? People would rather go where they are not considered "outsiders."

Church buildings are usually very beautiful and attractive, but often, when someone, out of the emptiness of his life, turns to the church for help, he runs into a member who is not loving. A young girl asked me one day, "What is the difference between the people who go to church and the people who don't?" Before I could answer another girl said, "The people who don't go to church are more loving than the people who do go to church."

For too long the "church" was aloof from the world. Conscientious leaders of today have discovered that God has loved the world all this time and sent His Son to redeem it (John 3:16–17). "God was in Christ reconciling the world to himself, not counting their trespasses against them, and entrusting to us the message of reconciliation" (2 Corinthians 5:19).

Many older people have told me that they are afraid of this "loving attitude" toward "sinners" because it seems "too much like condoning sin." They forget that Jesus always loved the sinner and thought of him *apart* from his sin.

Others are even more bewildered by leaders who go to the other extreme and practically join the man who has fallen in the gutter. One thing can be said for this man: he is not "holier than thou." Jesus wasn't aloof either; the sinners knew His love, but He never stooped to "sin with the sinner" to prove His involvement. In fact, He didn't have to *prove* His love. He was love.

Not only do many leaders feel impelled to *prove* their love involvement, but many are still reacting against the hardness of religious people who condemned the sinner along with his sin. Many church people are "turning to the world" before they have a message for that world and so misinterpret Christian involvement. That message is the same that Jesus chose for Himself at the beginning of His ministry: "The Spirit of the Lord is upon me, because he has anointed me to preach good news to the poor. He has sent me to proclaim release to the captives and recovering of sight to the blind, to set at liberty those who are oppressed, to proclaim the acceptable year of the Lord" (Luke 4:18–19; cf. Isaiah 61:1–2).

I am one of the "older ones" but I am not frightened about the Church at all. "The things which are being shaken are obviously things which *can* be shaken. They are revealed to be man-made, passing or temporal things by the fact that they are shaken. And they are being moved out of the way so that the things which cannot be shaken may remain."* The real Church is still the "Body of Christ." This modern time is the greatest day the Church has ever seen, for it alone has the message that the distraught world is waiting for.

When Mahatma Gandhi was asked for advice to Christians, one of the points he made was, "Practice the Sermon on the Mount without adulterating it or toning it down." I thought of this when I read comments about a recent book on the Sermon on the Mount, *Salt and Light.* A prominent churchman who should have been delighted with such a book said it was impractical and would not speak to the world today! But the secular press welcomed it: "Among the volumes of interpretations of the Sermon on the Mount, very few seem to provide much salt or light on the subject. The same clichés are used ceaselessly to cover the same parables in the same old way. But Eberhard Arnold has provided both salt and light on the teachings of Christ in this flavorful and enlightening book. This book constitutes a testimony of faith, something really rare in today's material-minded, dollar driven world. If your faith needs a shot in the arm, or heart, this book should provide it."

This is part of what these reviewers read:

* Anon., Enlargement of Hebrews 12:27.

The scribes and Pharisees had a firm conviction, a moral direction and an iron will. They were better than their reputation: they were morally upright, devout figures who commanded respect, men who felt deeply their responsibility for their people, for morals and religion. But what they lacked was the free spirit that blows from God. What they did not have was the gift of life from God, the life that must grow and bear fruit just because it is there. What they lacked was being filled with the Holy Spirit. What they lacked was God Himself.

Jesus brings a wholly different righteousness. He brings God's goodness because He brings God Himself, who encompasses everything and tolerates nothing isolated; the living God, who wants nothing but life; the God of riches, whose being consists in giving; the God of radiating light and flooding warmth. Only those who lose themselves in God have the new justice. Only where God Himself lives and works does this justice of the warmly pulsing heart take the place of the stony tables of the law.*

Jesus said the Christian should be salt and light in the world. And the world will know when the salt is there and when the light is there.

On the same night that the honored church leaders of that day could not enter the Roman court lest they be ceremonially defiled, but could lead in the

---

* E. Arnold, *Salt and Light,* trans. Society of Brothers (Rifton, N.Y.: Plough Publishing House, 1967), pp. 49, 50.

condemnation of Jesus, the Lord had met with His disciples to prepare them for the dark days immediately ahead. His message to them was, "Be of good cheer, I have overcome the world" (John 16:33), and he prayed for them and for us,

> I do not pray that thou shouldst take them out of the world, but that thou shouldst keep them from the evil one. They are not of the world, even as I am not of the world. . . . As thou didst send me into the world, so I have sent them into the world. . . . I in them and thou in me, that they may become perfectly one, so that the world may know that thou has sent me and has loved them even as thou hast loved me.
>
> John 17:15–23

Our discernment of Reality and life comes through our relationship with God and in *living His love*. His people are His Church on earth—to do His will—in every relationship with others.

Chapter 6

Can You Hold On?

The world is full of unappreciated blessings. Too many people do not know what of real value they have to hold onto. Self-pity lets many joys slip away.

We were a group of five women with retired husbands at home. Of course, we talked about husbands, especially retired ones. Suddenly one of the women, very attractive and an active church worker, burst out, "But, you know, I think I'll go crazy having a man underfoot all the time. I thought I loved him, but now I don't know if I do or not!"

It is amazing how many good churchwomen feel like this. Then they wonder why they feel blocked in their spiritual growth. It seems to be news to many active Christians that spiritual growth is advanced or hindered by success or failure in *human relationships*.

This does not mean that if we cannot "get along" with some people we cannot have relationship with God. Even Jesus did not "get along" with "church" people. The apostle Paul explained it well: "If possible, *so far as it depends upon you,* live peaceably with all" (Romans 12:18, italics added). We are responsible for our own redemptive attitudes toward other people.

So it is not only our relationship to *things* that must be reappraised at retirement time. And it is not only our relationship to God which should have been under continual appraisal all through the years, but husbands and wives may be forced to a reappraisal of their own relationship.

Now look again at that good churchwoman. Before her husband retired from his business she had her days in her own hands. She could work at her own pace without comments from anyone. She had her kitchen to herself without suggestions from a culinary novice. She could go and come freely without any argument. No one was at home feeling lonesome when she went to a women's meeting. She had been able and glad to prepare for her husband's homecoming each evening. Now all her accustomed freedom was gone. She felt penned in and penned up. A housewife cannot retire, but she has to be able to adjust.

Now consider that poor husband. He was no longer needed at his old place of work. They were getting along fine without him. And he was in the way at home! He had looked forward to leisure time; now he had it and he did not know what to do with it. He had enjoyed his wife in the years of evenings they had shared together. He could not understand what had happened to their relationship. Why should she suddenly think he was in the way? He began to wonder if he loved her at all. The more irritated she was with his presence the more insecure he felt. He did not even feel like turning to the other interests and hobbies he had been looking forward to. What a mess!

Before retirement troubles began, they had enjoyed praying together, but that had gone hollow on them now. They felt guilty about this, because they were sincere church people and believed that families should pray together. They were both frustrated.

This woman finally realized that she was thinking only of herself and that she was wallowing in self-pity. She had sense enough to ask the Lord to help her change her attitude. She began to think of her husband's dilemma and to understand his difficulty. As she patiently helped him find his way into fruitful interests she discovered a new freedom in her own life beyond anything she had ever known before. And they found a fellowship together in the Lord that was beyond the dream of any bride.

It is not too hard for a couple to get over retirement disruption if they have had a more or less successful marriage, but for those whose marriage has been an "endurance test" the way is really hard. Perhaps they stayed together "for the sake of the children." Now the children are gone, the new home for retirement is small, and the prospect for such togetherness is appalling. How can they take it? What is there to hold onto?

One such woman, an active church worker, said, "I've never had a happy day since my wedding. Now my husband is looking forward to a big golden wedding anniversary next year. I won't take that away from him, but as soon as it is over, I'm getting out!" The distraught woman half realized the incongruity of the situation so she came to me for help, even more than for sympathy. The story of her disappointments was long and varied. I asked

her about her husband's disappointments and how
was it that he could look forward to a golden wedding anniversary. Now her story really grew interesting. She said, "Why, I never thought about his
side of the story!" Then she began to think for the
first time of occasions when he really tried to
change in the very things for which she criticized
him. I asked, "What did you do on those occasions
when he tried to change?" She answered, "I guess I
squelched him." By that time she was sorry for her
husband instead of herself! When she started home
she said, "I am going back to make my husband
happy." Their fiftieth anniversary year has arrived,
a golden time to celebrate a new beginning.

Two teen-age girls were discussing their grandparents who still had an exciting relationship together. One girl said, "I had no idea that old people
could love each other so much." It is truly sad when
"old people" think the time for love and romance is
long since gone. Recently I had dinner with two
"old" love birds. They enjoy the extra time together since retirement. No wonder! She was wearing two rosebuds. I thought it was an anniversary.
It was just *Friday*. Every Friday of their married
life he has given her two rosebuds! (Now don't
count it against your husband if he doesn't express
his love that way. Mine doesn't either!)

It is really "old fashioned" to think that normal
people after fifty might just as well have separate
rooms, that longing for one another is a thing of the
past.

"While the general belief is that emotional ecstasy and eloquence are limited to early adult years, physicians with years of experience know that romance often is one of the colorful and energizing experiences of later life."*

"There is a unique kind of happiness ahead for the older husband and wife, if they can spend the final years of their lives together. It will not be a repetition of the honeymoon period, but something far richer and deeper. Like the honeymoon, however, it may be a time of discovering some new things in the personality of the beloved companion."†

With the change of circumstances after retirement there is indeed a period when two people must get acquainted again. If they accept this as an adventure a whole new future will open up to them.

Now is the time for the richest experience of real love. Romance is no longer a requirement for security in marriage, but is still a bonus in an abiding relationship. A husband's loving appreciation for his seventy-year-old wife still makes her heart beat faster.

It has been said that sex is a four-letter word spelled l-o-v-e. The intimacy of married love is now enriched by the gentleness that comes for a real appreciation of one another. The fears of younger married love are in the past. There is full freedom to enjoy a love that has been truly tested.

Any husband and wife who have loved each other

* Edward L. Bortz, M.D., *Creative Aging* (New York: The Macmillan Company, 1963), p. 132.
† Lulu S. Hamilton, *Your Rewarding Years* (New York: Bobbs-Merrill, 1955), p. 29.

through the years look back to especially precious moments. But they know that the deepest moments are not those of great romance but, rather, those times of greatest need when they shared sorrow and loss together, when they were even too tired to "emote." There are elements of reality in a relationship of tested love that exuberant beginning love has not yet tasted.

This is the kind of love the apostle Paul meant when he told husbands to love their wives as Christ loved the Church (Ephesians 5:25). The word for "love" that Paul used is not the Greek word for romantic love but for God-love, for Christ-love—*agape.* It denotes a *giving-love* which dynamically loses itself in the best welfare of the one loved. It does not ask, "What do I get?" but "What can I give?" It is rich and deep, never selfish. It gives a sense of new dignity to the one who gives and to the one who receives. Any woman would be delighted to "obey" a man who loves like that. This is a love not learned in a day. It takes time even to develop the capacity to receive this gift of God-love.

We never grow too old to love, and it is never too late to learn to love like this. No one need be bound by past loveless years. Any day can be a new beginning. It is this kind of love that turns eyes of faith and hope to the future and makes life worth living—at any age.

Not long ago I met a "grandma-age" woman in a church in Ohio. Every time I said to her, "How are you?" she answered, "I am so happy." There was such a conscious joy in her answer each time that I wanted to know more about her. I was surprised to find that most of her life had been full of disappointments and heartache. She had lost two husbands. She loved children but had never had any. There were long years of loneliness, but all these experiences only "stretched out spaces in her heart for joy."

When this dear lady was sixty-five she married a widower. On her wedding day she became a mother to one son and seven daughters, and grandmother to thirty grandchildren, with two more since then. She wrote, "Words cannot express my happiness with my family and I thank the Lord every day for my many blessings."

Another lovely thing about this woman is that she does not grasp her joy and hold it to herself. She gladly shares her husband with others. She leaves him free for his deep interest, an important agricultural project. When he was asked to accompany seventy-four head of cattle by air to India she was glad for his opportunity for service and travel. She said, "I would not have deprived him of such an opportunity for anything."

Love is the most practical thing in the world for any age. It is also the most Godlike, for God is love and no one can know God without knowing and acting love. You cannot be a hypocrite if you love, for God is working from the inside out in you.

Have you ever realized that your relationship with your mate is the test of your relationship with God?

Love is patient and kind; love is not jealous or boastful; it is not arrogant or rude. Love does not insist on its own way; it is not irritable or resentful; it does not rejoice at wrong, but rejoices in the right. Love bears all things, believes all things, hopes all things, endures all things.

                        1 Corinthians 13:4–7

Read this aloud to yourself, and then together, substituting *I* for *love,* and hear how it sounds! It may surprise you both. At any rate, it can give you the most specific faith in the fact that *love* is the commodity to which we are to hold on!

Chapter 7

Can You Let Go?

Mother's halo is gone! She lost it because she tried to fasten it on. While she tried to fasten it on she turned it into apron strings!

Nancy grew up abroad with a deep appreciation for her family. When she came to America to attend college she would write a few lines on her "home letter" each day. The other girls in the dorm taunted her about her being tied to her mother's apron strings, but she was sure she wasn't. After a while she found that the other girls were ashamed to express family love, that there was a cult of rebellion among these American young people. This puzzled her.

During the Second World War motherhood had a bad press for the first time in history. It was reckoned as "smother" love and unfortunately, in many cases, it was only too true. So many articles and books derided "smotherhood" and the immaturity of being tied to mother's apron strings that young people became ashamed to let family love be known. No one can measure the loss to the healthy family life of America by this thoughtless deriding of the family.

How could all this happen in a civilized land of plenty? Perhaps the condition of "plenty" had something to do with it. There has been a deliberate, even though unplanned, disruption of family life. We may not be able to do much about the rebellion, but we can see where we of the older generation gave some grounds for rebellion.

When young people speak frankly about what bothers them the most it seems that they are more irritated by parental *anxiety* than anything else. To young people I would explain the *reasons* for parental anxiety. But now we are looking at our side. This anxiety is nearly always about something that the young people are old enough to be responsible for themselves. In their irritation they rebel at not being given responsibility. "What's a mother to do?" The law for the transference of responsibility is: Never do for a child what he can do for himself. Do you remember back to the time when they were little?

Tommy had learned to tie his shoestring and was so proud of his achievement. Do you remember what happened on Sunday morning when you were in a hurry to get to church on time? Little Tommy was slow, of course. You interrupted his effort by exclaiming, "We'll be late—here, let me tie that string for you." Then one little thwarted fellow had a tantrum! You did not let go of your responsibility when he was able, however slowly, to take it on. That was the beginning.

How many times through the years did you say, "I can do it faster or better, let me do it for you"? Did they rebel or submit? (I hope they rebelled!)

I have discovered that young people do know right from wrong. If we let them take the real responsibility for their decisions they do very well.

That means that in any situation we do not pass judgment *before* they have a chance to.

When your daughter set up housekeeping near you, did you let her learn in the new life at her own speed? One mother snooped into her daughter's kitchen cupboards and bureau drawers to see how she was doing in her housekeeping arts. One father made his son come every morning and report on his sex life with his bride.

Perhaps you have not learned to let go. Then the day came when you were old and alone. Have you ever used the fact that you are her mother to play on your daughter's heart strings so she will do things for you, or to make her sacrifice her family responsibilities when you have other adequate arrangements for your life? Have you made her feel guilty and unappreciative when she did not do exactly as you suggested? If you have, you have turned a possible halo into apron strings.

One widow, a very active churchwoman, decided to move in with her youngest daughter. Why should she wait for an invitation? Wasn't it her "baby daughter"? She took charge of the kitchen, the shopping, and the care of the children to "help her daughter." Worst of all, she was very critical of her son-in-law. The daughter was constantly torn between loyalty to her husband and to her mother. Of course, the daughter got sick and landed in the hospital. Then the older brother intervened and got mother into a lovely home for senior citizens where she used all her energies in visiting the lonely people and became a real blessing to them.

Many couples say they would like to have a lone

parent live with them if the parent could adjust to another family. Actually the problem is not so much age as it is a problem of *self-centered interference*. One daughter said, "I'm glad to have my mother but I can't stand it for my children to hear her complaining and self-pitying." She loved her mother and she wanted the grandchildren to love her too, but they almost despised her. Why does this older woman interfere? She simply had never learned to let go and let others carry their own responsibilities.

There was the "old lady" who was the despair of every Sunday school teacher and every social group. Whenever she was present she took over the show by her cantankerous questions. There was also the widower, otherwise so gentle, who had very definite ideas on health and theology and who could break up any discussion group because he could not bear to listen to anyone else.

Entire churches are kept in an uproar by such garrulous "oldsters" who push their ideas onto everyone, and if they don't like the pastor they can really cause trouble! They may even form cliques which they call "prayer groups" to "preserve the purity of the church." Perhaps all these troublemakers really don't *want* to make trouble, and perhaps some would stop, if only someone could reach them and help them.

Of course, this aggressiveness into other people's lives is often the result of fears which have crept in unwittingly as life's responsibilities have receded. This means that the real meaning of love has slipped away in the darkness of fear, and the art of listening to another's need has been lost.

There are more people over sixty-five than ever before in history (over nineteen million in the U.S.). This is also a time when the wisdom of experience is needed to balance the overemphasis on the opinions of youth, just because they are *the youth*. Old age was once respected because it was old age, but that is no longer true. "Age" must now win respect. That should be good for us. Perhaps we need the advice: "Look and see, listen and hear."

One of the greatest needs today is for a listening ear. Most people have to pay for that blessing (to the psychiatrist). A handsome white-haired minister I know was sitting in the lobby of a big city hotel. A beautiful young woman came up to him and asked if she might talk to him. She began, "I've been wanting to talk to a minister. I am a call girl and I want to tell some minister that over eighty percent of the men who pay to spend the night with me never want to touch me, they just want someone to talk to. Please tell the wives to have a listening ear." All the world needs a listening ear.

As long as your hearing is not impaired, no matter what other handicap you might have, you can minister to people.

Luke tells us about two delightful old listeners (2:25–38):

Now there was a man in Jerusalem, whose name was Simeon, and this man was righteous and devout, looking for the consolation of Israel, and the Holy Spirit was upon him. And it had been revealed to him by the Holy Spirit that he should not see death before he had seen the Lord's Christ. And inspired by the Spirit he came into the temple; and when the parents brought in the child Jesus, . . . he took him up in his arms and blessed God . . . and blessed them. . .

And there was a prophetess, Anna . . . she was of a great age . . . eighty-four. She did not depart from the temple, worshiping with fasting and prayer night and day. And coming up at that very hour she gave thanks to God, and spoke of him to all who were looking for the redemption of Jerusalem.

What joy to have old people like that around.

If you enjoy watching younger people taking their own responsibilities without feeling rejected you have learned to let go—in order to be a blessing.

Chapter 8

Are You Alone?

In Paris I once bought a London *Times* and found this ad:

Help the Aged. Alone in a squalid room with only fear for company. Home is a tiny one-room basement flat that lacks adequate heating, lighting, plumbing, cooking facilities. No relatives nearby to care. No friends ever visit. Thousands and thousands of old people today are condemned to similar conditions. Even a welfare state cannot keep pace with the growing need.

The *Chicago Sun Times* carried an article: "Golden Years Often Tarnished." Almost half the old people in Chicago live in poverty. Chicago conditions reflect the plight of many of the more than nineteen million Americans over sixty-five, the source, generally, of the nation's major poverty group. The article added: "Poverty in old age is often no change to elderly Negroes, who have endured economic poverty all their lives."

Out of the midst of poverty, however, come some wonderful stories. In London an old couple living on a small pension in a basement loved beauty so much that they raised beautiful flowers in boxes in front of their basement flat. The flowers were so lovely in such an unexpected place that the Queen Mother came one day to see what this old couple had achieved.

The question is not what poverty does to you but what do you do with what little you have. Are you reaching out or sitting alone in self-pity?

I am thinking of an eighty-five-year-old man who was left alone by the death of his wife, but he did not sit around in self-pity. He continued in their home doing all the housework himself. A friend asked, "What do you do there all by yourself?" He answered, "Well, you know a woman's work is never done." For his own enjoyment as he did his housework, he began to sing the old Pennsylvania Dutch folk songs he had learned in his youth. Friends began to hear what he was doing. The word spread until he was called on to sing many of these songs on a coast-to-coast television program.

Being *alone* does not necessarily mean *loneliness*. Your condition depends more on how you get along with yourself than on how little you possess. If you have a great emptiness in your life, you are not only alone but lonely. If your security had been in dependence on others or in their dependence on you, then when left alone you are lonely. This is an impoverishment which all the poverty programs may never touch. Poverty of mind and soul is poverty indeed and loneliness indeed.

Withdrawal is never creative aloneness; it leads only to loneliness. It is easy to feel that one's own sorrow, loss, or destitution is unique. Fear of further hurt makes people vulnerable so they are tempted to isolate themselves from others. This is a loneliness that is a sickness. A sharing with others will soon reveal that no one is unique in his suffering. Sharing may even reveal that a neighbor has greater tragedy in his or her life.

There is always agony in the loss of a loved one, but maturity says this loss has to be accepted. Pearl Buck in *A Bridge for Passing* and Catherine Marshall in *To Live Again* describe their own agony in the loss of a loved one and how they found the way through suffering. But they *found* the way through.

When one of my friends came back to an empty house after the funeral of her husband she wrote, "I tried to pray, no words came, but the thought occurred to me that God didn't need words from me because Jesus and my friends were holding me up to Him. It was good to experience this nearness to God."

Those who know the Lord are never alone. Solitary times are opportunities to know Him in greater depth. In order to be free for this new level of being, all self-pity must be conquered. Anything that is of self-centeredness must be reckoned for the enemy it is. God cannot squeeze into a self-centered heart. His abundant grace awaits an open door. "Be still, and know that I am God" (Psalms 46:10).

If solitude becomes a part of one's life, it is not to be despised. In fact it may be worthy of being sought. If the solitude follows years in the midst of the modern "rat race," it may be a well-earned privilege.

The only question is, Do you have what my mother called mental furniture? If you cannot stand to be alone, if you must always seek diversion outside yourself, then your "house" is empty, you have no mental furniture. You will never have peace unless you can furnish your inner house.

Worse than emptiness is the possibility of the wrong kind of mental furniture. Some people are driven by crippling fears: of being ignored, of being forgotten, of being discredited, of not being appreciated. Such fears pull the shades and keep out the light that comes from fellowship with others. The person's worst self is penned up inside, where he has to live with himself. Such an old man was put out of a hospital recently because his tongue was poison to everyone. He is in a beautiful church home now where they have mercy on him, but their patience may have a limit also because of what he does to others living there.

No one wants to live in such misery, so "Peace of Mind" books written by Jew, Catholic, and Protestant all become best-sellers. But peace of mind never comes to the one who seeks it just for himself. It *is* crazy to nurture self-centeredness when it never leads to peace of mind or happiness. These qualities are a by-product of giving oneself to God and to others.

Helena Kruger is one of my favorite people because every moment with her is an inspiration. She never tells about the wealth her family must have given up when they escaped from Siberia in 1921. They emigrated to the United States in 1924 and found work on a Pennsylvania farm. She was so grateful to the church they found, and to God, that she offered, with her husband's blessing, to volunteer for relief service. During and after the Second

World War she served in Belgium, Austria, Italy, and the United States. Later she also served in Greece and Germany. Part of the time her husband joined her and in the last years, as a widow, she continued this service of love. She wrote me, "My Redeemer has led me through darkness and brightness. He has blessed me every day with love to live with neighbors."

If you could visit Lorah Plemmons near the Marshes of Glynn in Georgia you would know what I am talking about. She has given her life in service, but she does not have to be needed. She is almost always alone at near ninety. Both daughters live and teach in New England. The congregation of birds that live in her trees, a few choice friends who drop in for tea and laughter give her variety but she loves the time alone with God. "I'd rather be alone thinking about something beautiful," she says, "than to have company buzzing for nothing."

There are those who have learned Lorah's lesson, not through bereavement but from life. I am thinking of those who never married, mostly women. They have given themselves as teachers for other women's children as well as hundreds of professional and service jobs. I imagine the majority have wasted little time in self-pity; their lives have been full of many interests. When the years pass for them they are already trained to take care of themselves and others. Their lives are usually blessed with rich friendships.

Just being alone is not a tragedy. The greatest tragedy of all is to feel lonely in the midst of people, or even in the marriage relationship. If this kind of aloneness has been a habit of life, it is doubly important late in life to have one's inner life renewed.

Jesus says to us as well as to His early disciples: "If anyone wishes to be a follower of mine, he must leave self behind; he must take up his cross and come with me. Whoever cares for his own safety is lost; but if a man will let himself be lost for my sake, *he will find his true self*. What will a man gain by winning the whole world, at the cost of his true self?" (Matthew 16:24–26, NEB).

Pascal said, "To love your fellowman you must know him; to know God you must love Him." If you are in the darkness of loneliness, perhaps your way into light is to begin to know your neighbor and develop a capacity for love so that you can love God in a new way.

When you know God you are never alone. He waits for you.

Chapter 9

Do You Have Real Friends?

Over and over again "older people" say, "Nobody comes to see me and no one is interested in me any more." It is one thing if family members could come and do not, but the larger question is, Why don't you have friends?

It is often said that the best way to have friends is to be one. You see many people. Why are they not drawn to you?

Do you talk only about your ailments? Of course, real friends want to know how you are. It might even be "fun" to compare arthritic pains. But if your doleful story is always about your own pains, even your friends will come out of duty and stay as short a time as possible.

Undoubtedly, constant attention to one's pain makes the suffering worse. Being able to be interested in something else is a great help. I have a friend, a musician, who suffers at all times with arthritis, but she talks only about all the concerts and lectures she attends. She has more time for them than she ever had before. They keep her from dwelling on her pains.

Do you feel critical of other people? Bitterness of soul is poison to others, whether they realize it or not. It is double poision to you if you can think of nothing else. One woman who had been very active in the church, when hospitalized as an invalid, gave herself over to bitter criticism. Her family dreaded visiting her and others stayed away. One day her pastor could take it no more himself. He told her she could not blame people for not coming because they did not want to hear all her bitter complaints against the church and its members.

Another hindrance to real friendship, which I have seen in communities for senior citizens, is an underlying competition between people: a constant watching to see that others do not get more advantages or honors. As long as other persons are judged by one's own self-reference there can be no friendship. A self-centered person does not have real friends because he or she cannot be a friend to others.

Genuine friendship is blocked also by seeking out others for what they can do for us. One person who owns a car in the midst of many others who do not is in constant demand. Too many ask favors without consideration for the convenience of the car owner. I know such drivers who are truly unselfish and want to share but still at times cannot help but feel *used*. Friendships are not built on using another as if he were a mere convenience.

If you really feel friendless and want friends, there *is* a way to get them. The way begins with your genuine involvement with the other person. You may have failed thus far because you were thinking only of yourself. It is not only a saying, but it is true that to have friends you must be one. There must be many lonely people near you. One woman did her visiting by telephoning. She helped many lonely people pass their long hours.

If you have a joyous heart you can be a great blessing to shut-ins. Ask your pastor; he may be very glad for your help. Every time you have helped someone you have made a friend.

There may be others who have dropped former interests and feel helpless with time on their hands. There might be someone whose interest is the same as yours. Get together on this interest. If you help another to be restored to a former interest you will find a new excitement in life, too. Time shared is never monotonous, and growing friendships make life very worthwhile.

Of course, the best friend of all is the Lord Jesus Christ. What a thrill it must have been to His disciples when He said, "No longer do I call you servants, for the servant does not know what his master is doing; but I have called you friends" (John 15:-15).

If we have become truly God's friend, we will find human friends without undue effort on our part—and will not be often alone.

Chapter 10

Is Leisure a Joy or a Burden?

Leisure is more dangerous for the old than for the young, the late Dr. Alexis Carrol said. It is the kind of dangerous living some of us looked forward to. To live, as my husband and I do, in a seven-room bungalow surrounded by trees and hills looked like heaven to me. I immediately bought three rocking chairs at Goodwill Industries, one for the bedroom and two for our front porch. I remembered the woman who said that when she got to heaven she was going to sit, just sit, in a rocking chair for a thousand years, then for the next thousand years she would rock!

I haven't been to heaven yet, so once in a while I steal the time merely to sit in a rocking chair on the porch, go into neutral, and thank God for the beauty of His world. Then I am ready again for the work that waits to be done.

Going into neutral in a rocking chair once in a while is not the same as the effort to cover boredom or loneliness by sitting all day in front of the television screen. A young man said recently about his mother, widowed and recently retired from an engrossing professional life: "I am worried about my mother. She's losing interest in life, she just sits and listens to soap operas all day." This is letting go of life, which is deadening to all creative powers.

If there have been real interests and hobbies during the years, retirement will not bring burdensome hours of leisure but, rather, a thrilling opportunity for time with those interests.

Many discussions about hobbies to occupy time sound very artificial. Even in retirement they can be an escape from life. When the hobbies are finished for the day there is still time on a bored person's hands. Surely there must be something more satisfying.

I have been intrigued by the emphasis on "calling forth gifts" in the Church of the Saviour in Washington, D.C.* No member is assigned to any special task in their various missions. Each one must find his own call of God for the ministry in which he can serve with an abandon which leads to fulfillment. Many of their new areas of service have developed out of new creative possiblities which members have found in their own lives.

Each person faces the question, "Is there within me a strength that lets me be unafraid? Can I allow myself to be present to another because I can trust my response and know that I am able for whatever comes? All of life puts that question. Can I be present to it, or have I so little trust in my inner resources that I am fearful of hurt, fearful of loss, guarding myself—not daring to lose my life, and therefore never finding it?"

---

* See Elizabeth O'Connor, *Journey Inward, Journey Outward* (New York: Harper & Row, 1968), p. 28.

Whenever anyone in the Church of the Saviour finds what his very own ability and contribution are, he has heard his call and knows he is chosen by God. "Life becomes his vocation." Any person who does not find this individual call is the one easily controlled and manipulated by the crowd. It may well be a "religious crowd" but it is nonetheless a crowd.

Gordon Cosby, pastor of the church, emphasizing the need for this call, says:

If our potential is blocked and has found no creative channels in which to flow, then what we feel in the presence of another is envy—only a perplexing pain or deadness. We will have no praise of another—no joy in another. Instead, we will turn away and in subtle ways seek to destroy another. This is why we cannot get on with the business of loving unless we are discovering our own gift.*

This sounds like the vocational guidance search of youth but it is important at any age. If you never found this opportunity for fulfillment, a vocation that was a whole of life, that's too bad, but it is still not too late. So it is high time you start. A job or a profession is only part of this kind of vocation. You can retire from a job or a profession, but you don't retire from this vocation; you are just turned loose in it under the power of the Spirit.

Perhaps every retirement home or community

* *Ibid.*, p. 109.

should start each person out on such a search. It is
true that plenty of activities are provided, but new-
comers must fit into what is already planned. If every person were directed in this personal search for
his own gifts, a whole new future should open up to
him. A few people find this kind of fulfillment, but
the majority seem to be just a part of the crowd.

In the early years of the school system of Gary,
Indiana, even the small children went from room
to room for different classes, just as in college. On
the way from room to room the children passed by
windowed rooms in front of which loitering was encouraged. Some would stop in front of the carpen-
ter shop, others in front of the printing shop, or the
sewing room, or the cooking room, or the art room.
As a child's interest grew in any area he was encouraged to pursue that interest in the search for his
own gifts. This process of a search for individual
gifts is as important at seventy as at seven.

Don't be surprised at anything. Who knows? You
might be a Grandma Moses. She began painting at
seventy-nine. I understand that a store in New York
received her famous jellies with some of her early
art work for display and sale. They advertised only
the jellies to their later consternation.

In a day when the individual "personal man"
feels lost in the "impersonal organization man" the
period of so-called retirement may be a time of re-
birth into a whole new flowering of your own possibilities.

We are never, in God's sight, supposed to be lost
in the crowd. And Jesus meant the abundant life
He promised to be ours all our days. Through the

Holy Spirit "there are varieties of gifts, but the same Spirit; and there are varieties of service, but the same Lord; and there are varieties of working, but it is the same God who inspires them all in every one" (1 Corinthians 12:4–6).

You may have even a greater surprise if you seek for your individual gifts under the guidance of the Spirit. You may be called upon to do things you think you cannot do. A dear friend of mine wrote, "The Lord has never called me to a job my size, and I am forever being stretched." You must take this into account when you search for you own gift.

I remember Bakht Singh of India in his early ministry as an evangelist. We were in the same national Youth Conference together. The microphone was not working, but it did not matter, for Bakht Singh's voice carried to everyone in the large auditorium. The surprise was that when he had become a Christian, on a boat en route to Canada to study engineering, he had been terribly shy and his voice was no more than a magnified whisper. When he felt God's call to preach he knew his limitations but he trusted God to meet his need. God gave him a strong voice and the courage to give the message already in his heart. He has since had a worldwide ministry.

God has a special ministry for everyone. If you have not found yours yet you now have the leisure to find it. Start looking and your leisure time will become a joy.

Chapter 11

What Can You Do?

Dr. Joseph H. Peck discovered that he had never really retired, he had merely changed the nature of his work. He said:

It is my firm belief that every man was born with some latent ability and the desire to follow some star of destiny; ninety per cent of us, however, lose sight of this goal somewhere between the ages of fifteen and thirty. And though we forget it entirely during our working years, that early spark of ambition remains hidden in our subconscious and can be rekindled easily once we sit down to take stock of ourselves, as every man should before he reaches retirement.

Make up your mind to it, as soon as you step down from your life's work you must be born again. That's the meaning of leisure.*

In retirement there is time to experience the joy of being alive and for doing things for the sheer fun of doing them.

If your church is an important part of your life, that will be a good place for you to begin. See what

---

* *Let's Rejoin the Human Race* (Englewood Cliffs: Prentice-Hall, 1963), p. 143.

is needed there that you might do. There may not be offices or paid jobs for you, but every church has people in it who need friends. This is true in your community, too. Keep an eye open for the needs of other people.

One church in a large city could not get the young marrieds into any of the activities which they were equipped to provide for them. The couples said they could not afford baby-sitters. It so happened that there was an unusually large group of older people in this church. Many of them felt unwanted and unneeded. A plan was set in motion for the older folk to "adopt" some young couple and give free baby-sitting as their service for the church. This service was offered also for other occasions outside church activities. In appreciation for such love, the young couples could not be kept away from the church!

The Federal Government wants grandparents, too. They employ such grandparents in hospitals, homes for the mentally retarded children, homes for dependent children, and in other institutions. Some two thousand, five hundred Foster Grandparents are employed in eight-nine institutions across the country. They work up to twenty hours a week and earn from $1.40 to $1.77 per hour. Each grandparent is trained in an intensive orientation program. Then they go to provide the loving care these children would otherwise never have. They say that the Foster Grandparents get as much joy out of this as the children do. If you are interested in becoming a Foster Grandparent write to Administration on the Aging, 330 Independence Ave., Washington,

D.C. 20201. Of course, you don't have to be married to be this kind of grandparent; neither do you have to be a woman. Grandfathers are needed, too.

If you love to travel, retirement is the time for that. On my trip to the Middle East with a tour group, we had three people over eighty in our party. And they never brought up the rear either! I said I would not ride a camel in Egypt because I never want to be thought of as a typical tourist. But all the others did, including the eighty-year-olds, so I got on one, too. I drew a young balky fellow which did everything but throw me! At least I could say that at seventy-three I kept up with the eighty-year-olds!

Bob Belmont wrote a book about travel for older folk: *How to Retire without Money* (Gallant Books). He says his kind of retiring begins at twenty-one by always doing what one enjoys doing. He did and he found how to travel and support himself at the same time. This delightful book is about his experiences and also the experiences of his friends. There are plenty of other travel books available, even on how to travel in Europe on five dollars a day.

Of course, there are many crafts, collecting, endless kinds of hobbies, each to his own interest. For suggestions galore you will find great help in *101 Ways to Enjoy Your Leisure* (A Retirement Council Publication, One Atlantic St., Stamford, Conn.) with full data on how to get all the information you need.

You need not push yourself. Take time to consider your inner longings and the opportunities before you. If you truly trust God you can take each day as it comes and a new life will surely open up to you as it did to Ervin Stuntz of Indiana. Ervin was a farmer who loved God, people, farming, and his sawmill work. In planning for retirement he bought one hundred and forty-eight acres of "useless" land. It was blow sand and marshes. He immediately reforested sixty acres in pines which developed into a Christmas tree business that gives them their living. Each year ten thousand more trees are planted.

The Girl Scouts began to come there for camping, then the Boy Scouts, the 4-H clubs, and other youth groups. Ervin decided they needed better facilities. So he cleared space for seven campsites. One main camp is near a lake which Ervin made. He ordered it to be made as large as two thousand dollars would permit. It covers one and one-half acres and is kept stocked with bluegill and bass.

Then Ervin decided that a hall was needed. So in 1965 he took six thousand dollars out of his business and built a hall with kitchen and facilities. The large fireplace at one end and the hand-painted picture done by a friend make the hall very inviting. Still more room was needed, especially for family reunions, so in 1967 he built a barn for overflow crowds.

No charge is ever made for youth groups of any kind. Ervin even pays the electric bills and the insurance. Church groups are also not charged. Family reunion groups pay only a small fee.

Ervin and Cecil Stuntz are not rich in money. They sell their Christmas trees at Christmas, but they make Christmas for others the whole year through. I have never met any two people more excited about life. They are appreciated, too. Among other awards, Ervin has been made an honorary Girl Scout. I think he is proudest of that. Many people have not changed professions upon retirement, they have simply gone to another place. School-teachers often continue as substitute teachers in another location. Many "retired" people have joined the Peace Corps and have found adventure and helpfulness around the world. Whether the job changes, or the place, age is not the determining factor, but inner spirit and courage and a sense of adventure.

Grandma Ikenberry was an active, loved queen of her large family until her death at one hundred and seven. When she was ninety, her son, who lived in Indiana, said to her, "Mother, I am coming back to Virginia to visit you on your birthday every year, as long as you live." When she was one hundred, this son said to her, "Mother, from here on I think you will have to visit me!"

"Mother Garst" is the inspiration of people all over Roanoke. She's eighty-five, the mother of nine, grandmother of twenty-seven, and great grandmother of thirteen. Although she has moved into an apartment in Friendship Manor, she still goes downtown on the bus two days a week to teach her piano students. Two days she quilts with the ladies in the Manor and the rest of the time she cares for the Manor flowerbeds. Forty-year-olds find it difficult to keep up with her. And no matter what happens, "Mother Garst" is always joyous in the Lord.

Recently the American composer Aaron Copeland was interviewed on television. He said a lady once told him: "Do something new when you are old so you aren't in competition with yourself when you were young." My guess is that after seventy you need never be in competition with yourself or anyone else. Satisfaction from the fulfillment of your years can take the place of the pressures of competition.

We are not to sit around waiting to die; we are to live life to the full as we never dreamed of doing before.

Chapter 12

What Are You Learning?

To get a new idea at any age is a thrilling experience. To get it in later years is almost like regeneration. The fountain of youth is still considered mythical but the possibilities of rejuvenation seem inexhaustible.

As a retired person you have made many adjustments socially and economically. You may even have come through difficult crises of faith, but have you kept a growing edge on your intellectual development! There is still plenty to learn and you may have more time now than ever before.

Even if you are confined to one place because of ill health or lack of funds you need never be penned in. There is the whole wide world of books. In the early days of television, publishers and educators were afraid book sales would suffer. That has not happened. There are more books published and sold today than ever in history. If you cannot afford to buy them you can find them free in your public library or church library.

Anyone can educate himself by careful reading. If you have difficulty in directing your reading you might find help and stimulation by joining one of the Great Books Discussion Groups. There are approximately thirty-five hundred of them in the

United States and Canada. If there are none near you, why not start one yourself?*

A group working together on the same reading has the advantage of lively discussion after doing each week's "homework." In such a discussion group you are not sharing ignorances, you are sharing discoveries.

Not only the reading, but the discussion may be a new discipline. Many persons have never learned this discipline. They think any group is merely a forum for them to expound their own theories. A young man, a very good teacher, was asked to teach a Sunday school class of older people. He enjoyed the experience until several older folk took over session after session to expound their pet themes on social and political issues no matter how irrelevant their words were.

Real fellowship can grow out of creative discussion groups. A pattern may be set for the sharing of ideas on matters which are not so vital to certain people so that when important issues arise everyone has learned how to be fair to those of differing opinions. (This procedure would certainly be a godsend to many church groups.)

A minister said recently, "If we can't disagree in the church where can we do it?" The church is a good place to learn how to disagree without breaking relationship, but few have availed themselves of the opportunity to do this. Somehow it seems easier

* Write to Great Books Foundation, 5 South Wabash, Chicago, Illinois 60603.

to learn it in so-called secular groups, where the issues are less personal.

If you have sight problems or are blind you need not be left out of the reading or discussion experience. Tapes and records as well as Braille books are available for you to "read" with your ears or your fingers and you can be an integral part of any sharing group.

Whether you have the privilege of being in a reading group or not, the whole world is before you in the wide scope of available books. Those of us who have always loved to read, know already that a stimulating learning experience can be up ahead when we settled down in a comfortable chair and open a new book.

When you have a new book "going," it is much the same as having an interesting visitor in the house. Books are friends—dependable teaching friends in the main, and as in friendship it is just as important for the reader to "give" to the book as it is for the book to "give" to the reader. A well-written book, with substance in its pages—whether it is fiction or nonfiction—requires your participation, too. Think while you read and you will become personally involved with the author in what he has to say. Good books can change your life from boredom to enjoyment and take you into a whole new realm of learning. The extra bonus will be that you will become better company for your friends.

Chapter 13

Do You Understand Your Bible?

The Bible is the world's best-seller, but unlike many best-sellers it is also the most important reading you can do. It is also the least understood book. Sunday school lessons are very important, but perhaps the one unfortunate result of the Sunday school is the weekly study of only a small portion of the Bible without a proper study of the context of that portion. Many people read the Bible, but they do not really know what they read.

The deacon Philip was called away by the Spirit from a successful evangelistic meeting to go south on a desert road where he found an Ethiopian man, a minister to the queen, in his chariot reading the book of Isaiah. Philip stepped up to him and asked, "Do you understand what you are reading?" The man answered, "How can I, unless someone guides me?" And he invited Philip to sit in the chariot with him. Beginning with the Scripture which he was reading, Philip told him the Good News of Jesus. When they came to some water, the man asked for baptism. And the deacon baptized him (Acts 8:-26–39).

We wish we could have heard Philip's explanation that brought this response in such an important man. But we can see that the explanation must

have been good news and that the Ethiopian
queen's minister was open to new ideas.

It seems that the hardest area for people to get
new ideas in is their relation to the Bible. Philip
said the central truth of the Scripture was in Jesus
Christ. Jesus himself said the same thing to the
Pharisees, who were the theologians of His day, but
they missed the heart of the Scripture because they
did not accept Him. Jesus said there is a right way
and a wrong way to read the Bible. He said that
reading the Scripture was a matter of life [and
death?], and life means relationship. It is much
more than ideas. It is much more than ideas *about*
God. The Jewish scholars knew *about* God but they
did not *know* God. This is the reason they could not
recognize Jesus as the revelation of God.

It is very easy for us, even today, to make the
same mistake in reading the Bible, especially if we
do not use the "glasses" Jesus and Philip recom-
mended—to see all the Bible in relation to Jesus
Christ as its center, the true revelation of what God
is. Unless we come into a *personal relationship with
God* we also have missed the point of the Scripture.

So many conscientious "older people" think they
have to *defend* the Bible. Then other conscientious
people with different views enter into an argument
and soon there is no evidence of love among the
"brethren." And all have forgotten that Jesus said
that love is the first test of orthodoxy! (Read John
13:35; 1 Corinthians 13; and 1 John 4.) Love is a
personal concept, not merely an idea-word to be
tossed about.

We do not have to protect God's Word, we only *witness* to it.

Perhaps we need to learn to read the Bible. Only those who come with open hearts to learn anew from God can find the great truth revealed in His Word. Most people who have trouble, or make trouble, stumble over words and see words only. But John tells us that Jesus is the *Word*. He is the Light of life. His Spirit will "light up" our minds as we read the words to find the Word (John 1:14).

Whenever we take verses alone we can prove anything by the Bible. Many people do this, then try to prove that their ideas are right by using, or misusing, certain texts. In small portions of Scripture we see ideas only. Even when the ideas are true we have not read enough or found enough. The one who merely wants to prove himself right is not open to new ideas. But the one who seeks to find the Word of God for him is open to new ideas from the Lord. The Holy Spirit can have a good time with a mind open to God.

It is very hard to know the difference sometimes between a stubborn defense of one's own interpretation of the Bible and the deep conviction that comes from a real relationship with God. But in time we can tell the difference. The stubborn defender is very unloving to all who disagree with him. The one who has relationship with God is merciful toward those who differ from him. Above all he is willing to listen to people before he asks them to learn from him.

In the Old Testament we find the story of the

beginnings of God's relationship with man. God, the Creator of all, took the initiative toward man. This was as true in the Old Testament as in the New, but the Old Testament story is largely heartache and trouble on man's side. The majority of "God's people" were so slow to understand and obey God.

Nearly every time we find wonderful statements of God's outreach to man we find the statement followed by the fact of disobedience. "For the eyes of the Lord run to and fro throughout the whole earth, to show his might in behalf of those whose heart is blameless toward him" (2 Chronicles 16:-9). But the king to whom this message was given disobeyed God.

However, there were those who were faithful to God: Abraham had faith in one God when all others were idolaters; Moses stood alone with God in leading the Israelites out of slavery; David the king loved God and knew how to praise Him, but when he acted "with Bathsheba" like other kings of his day he knew guilt which they never felt and, more than that, he knew how to find forgiveness. Through all the days of mass disobedience the voice of God was heard through the amazing prophets. They perceived God's thought and spoke His words of warning and of *hope*.

All these Old Testament men who were faithful to God lived as men of God in spite of their environment and in spite of great suffering and misunderstanding. They indeed rose far above the culture of their day. Their work and message gives us the real background of the New Testament. But none understood fully about God, so it was necessary for God to send His Son so men would truly know what God is like.

To know about Jesus, the Son of God, and to feel the impact of His life as revelation, read each Gospel through in one sitting. The events and ideas will not stand out so much as the *Redeemer himself* in His infinite love for all in spite of the fact that the Bible students of His day saw to it that He was crucified.

To grasp some of the glory of the resurrection power released in the lives of the first Christians through the Holy Spirit, read the pattern-breaking story of the book of Acts—in one sitting.

"The Lord added to their number day by day those who were being saved" (Acts 2:47). This was the beginning of Christian churches. It is a surprise to see in the Letters (Epistles) to the churches that they had the same problems we have in our churches today. Read the whole of this part of the New Testament to see the work of the Spirit and the patience of the love of God as He worked through Peter and Paul and others to lead the people into a growing experience of God.

If you want to watch for something to hold your attention for years to come watch especially in the early Church how the transition was made from a small Jewish group into a large number of people, mostly Gentiles. See how God led, through the Spirit, in dropping off things merely cultural and into ways *distinctly Christian*. Their transition experience into a different culture can give us a pattern of what to hold onto and what to let go of our old ways.

The Good News of Jesus Christ is just as relevant today as it was in Paul's day. As we come to His Word with open minds and hearts He will speak to us today as He did to those of Bible times. What a joy to know Him and to hear Him!

Chapter 14

Do You Know the Secret?

The Gospel was first gossiped (this is still the best evangelistic method ever tried). And the gossip was about a secret that could be told. It is called a secret because it was unknown until Jesus lived and died and rose again and sent the Spirit to be our life and teacher.

Although this secret has been clearly revealed in the New Testament and was Paul's greatest theme, still the majority of Christians do not seem to know it.

Even today people talk about the Bible in the same way many of the scholars did in Jesus' day, as if it were an end in itself. This is the reason that John had to emphasize the fact that Jesus is the Word of God: "He came to his own home, and his own people received him not . . . . And the Word became flesh and dwelt among us . . ." (John 1:-11, 14–18).

We have already seen the mere membership in a church is not enough to insure a healthy spiritual life. But even in an active church oriented in loving service this great secret may be overlooked. The values of fellowship and mutual concern are simply not enough when the hardest tests of life come. Jesus said He would not leave us desolate. Now there is a *deeper relationship* possible with God. The po-

tential of this deeper relationship is part of the secret, but this secret is greater than even our relationship with God. It is the *plan for all of life.* "For
God has allowed us to know the secret of his plan,
and it is this: he purposes in his sovereign will that
all human history shall be consummated in Christ,
that everything that exists in Heaven or earth shall
find its perfection and fulfillment in him" (Ephesians 1:9–10, Phillips).

This is the greatness of our Lord: He is central
in all history and in all life. No wonder the apostle
Paul could say, "When I think of the greatness of this
great plan I fall on my knees before God the Father"
and on his knees Paul reveals the rest of God's secret
for his children: "and I pray that out of the glorious
richness of his resources he will enable you to know
the strength of the Spirit's inner reinforcement—that
Christ may actually live in your hearts by your faith.
. . . May you be filled through all your being with
God himself!" (Ephesians 3:14–19, Phillips).

Paul wrote to the Colossians, "For I am a minister of the Church by divine commission . . . that I
might fully declare God's Word—that *sacred mys-
tery which up till now has been hidden* in every age
and every generation, but which is now as clear as
daylight to those who love God. They are those to
whom God has planned to give a vision of the full
wonder and splendor of his secret plan for the sons
of men. And the *secret is simply this: Christ in
you!* Yes, Christ *in you* bringing with him the hope
of all the glorious things to come" (Colossians 1:-
25–27, Phillips).

This is such a practical secret that it is strange

that devout people could ever think that church membership only, or church activity only, or even doctrinal belief only could be enough.

Church membership might be merely a social relationship, leaving one stranded when alone. Such a member can be an unconscious leaner, dependent on the group for strength with no means of support when he is alone.

Participation in church activities and in service to others will bring a sense of fulfillment, but if there is nothing more, when the activity must cease, the person will feel lost and unwanted. This is the reason so many of our best workers are so frustrated when they can no longer serve in the same way. Active participation, as important as it is, is not enough.

A "faith" that is only doctrinal belief may give security for a time, but the time may come when one feels he has to *hold* his faith. Whenever anyone gets protective of his faith he gets hard and unloving. Such "faith" brings no witness to the love of God. In definition it may be all right, but definitions can leave one cold and lonely.

Our real faith is in a *Person,* in Our Lord Jesus Christ. He is knowable and can not only save us from our sins but wants to dwell within us to give us new life indeed. The wonder of it is that the secret which the apostle Paul found is ours, too: that Christ is alive in us now and we can have the same relationship with God and the same power available for our daily lives.

This is the open secret for anyone.

Chapter 15

What about Your Prayer Life?

When you know the Secret of Life—Christ in you—you will never be left stranded, no matter what happens to you. Even though your body changes with the years and many activities cease, this inner life can become more real all the time.

The apostle Paul wrote to the Corinthians, "So we do not lose heart. Though our outer nature is wasting away, our inner nature is being renewed every day" (2 Corinthians 4:16). There is a growing security in this relationship with Christ. Reading His Word is listening to His voice. In the quietness of the hours when you are seemingly alone, you can know His thought for you in your every need. Speaking to Him is your natural response in this growing friendship together. Communion with Him becomes more spontaneous with the passing of every day.

You may find something you did not discover in your very busy days. This listening to Him and looking to Him in worshipful response is really prayer. Words become almost incidental, posture becomes irrelevant. It is relationship which counts. We are His children and He is our Father.

Many people think of prayer only in terms of set times for talking to God. Some have even grown proud of the amount of time they have spent in Bible study and prayer or they have condemned themselves when circumstances cut down their set time for "devotion." It is very easy to become legalistic about the forms and frequency of prayer and to forget the *communion*.

Disciplines in the religious life have their value, but so far as discipline is concerned faithful devotees of other religions have the same experience—using other words and other forms. Without a *personal* relationship with God which is uniquely possible through Christ your prayer life may not be more effective than theirs.

The test of our faith comes when all of life's securities disappear. When our securities go, religion which is only form turns out to be empty indeed. We are like thirsty persons trying to drink out of empty cups. This is even more tragic if we started out with a personal relationship with God and let it dwindle into form only. Such people are described in 2 Timothy 3:5–7. They hold the form of religion but deny the power of it. These people can always be spotted because they "listen to anybody and can never arrive at a knowledge of the truth." The reason for this is that discernment comes through the Spirit of God and they have nothing left but an empty vessel.

This is what happened to the Galatian Christians. Paul asked them, "Did you receive the Spirit by works of the laws, or by hearing with faith? Are you so foolish? Having begun with the Spirit, are you now ending with the flesh?" (Galatians 3:2–3).

This does not mean that forms and symbols in

religion are not important. They can be very meaningful and spiritually suggestive. But if they are forms only, they bring spiritual emptiness.

This emptiness will show up first in one's prayer life. Just as a broken relationship between husband and wife shows up in broken communication, so it is in our relationship with God.

If you feel uneasy about your prayer life you have reason to be encouraged. The very fact that you are uneasy or miserable is evidence that you are walking in the light. "Live then as children of the light . . . . For light is capable of 'showing up' everything for what it really is" (Ephesians 5:8, 12, Phillips).

Praying that is more than mere form is definitely related to daily living. Our relationship with God is all tied up with our relationship to others. After we have been unloving toward someone, or impatient, or resentful, that hard or empty feeling we get when we try to pray is God's way of telling us that we are missing *His* way. By confession to God and to that someone, we can get back on the love path and again find a real sense of personal fulfillment instead of that devastating frustration.

Pastors and others who have had a fruitful public ministry in the church often experience an emptiness in their private worship. Dwight L. Moody said some ministers were lame because their public praying leg was longer than their private praying leg. This does not necessarily mean that their public ministry was empty. We may come to God for a blessing for others before we know how to come to Him fully for a blessing for ourselves.

Too many church workers feel let down on retirement because they have grown to depend upon the inspiration of their public prayers and they are inadequate in their own private relationship to God. Hobbies or big doses of television will never satisfy as a substitute for a personal living relationship with God. If you feel a bewilderment or lostness, recognize it as God's call to you for a renewal of relationship which will make private communication a joy.

Of course, there are those who, in all their lives, have never come into a living relationship with God, who have never prayed except in moments of despair. To them God seems to be dead, and they wish He weren't. But no one is too old to rediscover Him. So far as God is concerned we never have any time but *now*. And He always comes in wherever He is let in.

One day the disciples of Jesus asked Him to teach them to pray (Luke 11:1–13). They had just seen Him in prayer and they recognized that His prayer life had a quality unknown to them. Jesus first told them a story. A man had an unexpected guest at midnight. To understand this story we need to know that it was the custom of that country to offer food to a guest no matter what time he arrived. But this host had no prepared food on hand. So he went to his neighbor to borrow bread. With all his family asleep in the same room with him, the neighbor did not want to be bothered, but he finally had to yield to the request. He gave, but he was an *unwilling giver*.

Then Jesus told about an earthly father who

gives good food to his children when they are hungry. This father is a *willing giver*. The main point Jesus made is in His next statement; "If you then . . . know how to give good gifts to your children, *how much more* will the Heavenly Father give the Holy Spirit to those who ask Him?" God is the *gracious giver*. He gives even more than is asked, He gives the all-inclusive gift, the Holy Spirit.

The disciple's request was to learn to pray, and Jesus' answer was that the Holy Spirit through whom our relationship with God is established is the secret to vital prayer (Luke 11:1–13).

Then Jesus gave His disciples a pattern for prayer. This prayer, which we call the Lord's Prayer, has become so familiar to us that we are in constant danger of using it as a vain repetition. It would take more than a lifetime to search its depths.

The prayer which Jesus gave begins with the Gracious Giver, the Heavenly *Father* and not with man's needs. When we begin prayer with our attention on the great God who is our Father, we are truly brought to our knees in worship.

No one has described this prayer better in a few words than William Barclay:

The second part of the prayer is the most comprehensive prayer that men were ever taught to pray.
Let us sit down its three petitions;
Give us this day our daily bread.
Forgive us our debts as we forgive our debtors.

Lead us not into temptation, but deliver us from evil.

The first of these three petitions is a prayer for our present need. The second of them is a prayer for our past sin. The third of them is a prayer for our future welfare and goodness. These three short petitions take life, past, present and future and lay it before God.

But these three petitions do even more than that. When we pray the first of them, the prayer for daily bread, we think of *God the Father,* the Creator and Sustainer of all of life. When we pray the second of them, the prayer for our forgiveness, we think of *God the Son,* the Saviour and redeemer of all mankind, and of us. When we pray the third of them, the prayer for future help to live without sin, we think of *God the Holy Spirit,* the Guide, the Helper and the Protector of all life. These three petitions bring us face to face with Father, Son and Holy Spirit. Within their narrow compass, and with their astonishing economy of words, these three brief petitions take the whole of life to the whole of God.*

After such a prayer with its implications of constant relationship with God under all circumstances, no wonder the Church added the ascription of praise, *For thine is the Kingdom and the power*

* *The Beatitudes and the Lord's Prayer* (New York: Harper & Row, 1968), pp. 157–158.

and the glory (cf. 1 Chronicles 29:10–13). The
Amen is our own signature to the prayer and our
renewed commitment of life to the Heavenly
Father and His gracious will.

No matter what you consider the status of your
prayer life you can begin a new or renewed relationship with the God of love this very day because
He is alive and waits to communicate with you.

Through prayer we are the agents of the Creative
Spirit in this world. Prayer can even be a vocation.
Making prayer a vocation is no limp resignation to
fate; it is a total concentration on the total interests
of God. It is genuine, active partnership with God.
Prayer is a very special ministry open to invalids,
but it is a privilege and responsibility for every
Christian.

If you want to be a witness for Him, your prayer
life can be your proving ground.

Chapter 16

What Is Your Witness?

We cannot avoid it. As long as we live we witness to something or to someone. Is your witness to frustration, despair, cynicism, and hopelessness or is it to hope, courage and to the One who is with us at all times?

Many Christians who want to "witness" think only of a witness in *words*. Sometimes they talk until they are obnoxious, driving people away. It is unfortunate when such people say they represent the Lord Jesus Christ, for they do not represent Him, they represent their own egos!

There are times when only our living counts and words are in the way. "Likewise you wives, be submissive to your husbands, so that some, though they do not obey the word, *may be won without a word by the behavior of their wives,* when they see your reverent and chaste behavior" (1 Peter 3:1). One's witness begins with one's own *life*. The old saying is true, "What you do speaks so loudly I cannot hear what you say." The life of the witnessing person always counts first before words can begin to count.

When new life in Christ comes to a person, it is so wonderful that it usually bubbles over. This is fine and has its own charm in a new Christian just as it has for new lovers. An overflowing heart brings a real witness because of its joyous spontaneity. But

there is a witness of maturity which is also an overflowing out of one's own experience, although it is
more than an overflow. The mature witness is determined by the readiness of the one to whom it is
given. If the other person may be repelled by your
words and if you are truly mature, you will be satisfied to *live* your witness without words until words
are acceptable or even asked for.

Some people have a set witness: "What the Lord
has done for me." They say the same thing to everyone. They feel they have performed their duty
when they have told their story. One such woman
"witnessed" to her sister who was a missionary in
India in a church other than her own. When she
finished her witness to her missionary sister, she
said, "You can accept my witness or go to h——."
This was a witness to her own stubborn, hard self-
centeredness and not to a loving Lord.

Many with a set witness just do not know any
better. One student in Seminary cornered everyone
possible in order to tell what the Lord had done for
him. The Lord *had* done a real work in his life, but
people grew tired of his story and tried to avoid
him. This bothered him but he had no idea what to
do about it. One day in class he asked for criticism,
and got it! His classmates expected him to be hurt
by their frankness, but he had no time for that. He
was too busy trying to figure out where he had
been failing in his witnessing. That afternoon the
young man stopped me in the hall and said, "I have
just discovered where I have been failing. I have
been witnessing to *my* experience instead of to my

Lord." That was the beginning of fruitful witnessing for this man who truly loved the Lord.

Jesus is the perfect example of mature witnessing. He had more to tell about His experience with the Heavenly Father than any man who ever lived but His witness was always gauged by His listener's readiness to hear.

Jesus had the divine wisdom to discern the real need and spiritual hunger of those who came to Him. He also had the loving skill to do that which would lead them to be ready for the message which would be the most helpful to them.

The most unlikely person for Jesus to witness to was a Samaritan woman. According to custom, a good man would not open conversation with a strange woman as He did with her. She was also a woman with a bad reputation and that made it even worse. More than all that, she was a Samaritan and the Jews had a strong race prejudice against the Samaritans. Nevertheless Jesus started a conversation with her and broke all the barriers (John 4:-1–30). Finally, to *this* woman Jesus could explain the meaning of true worship and to *her* He could identify himself for the first time as the Messiah. What's more, this woman became a great witness for the Lord, and the people who had known her before listened to her words and came to hear Him.

The story of the blind man in the ninth chapter of John is another illustration of how Jesus met a man's need and waited to witness more fully until the man was ready to receive it. After the man grew in courage to witness to what had happened to him and was even cast out of the synagogue for "insolence," Jesus sought him out and introduced himself as the *Son of man*. The man, once blind, was now ready and he exclaimed, "Lord, I believe."

When God has done so much for us it is always harder to withhold words than it is to say them. But as we grow in the Spirit and away from self we grow into a greater understanding of others, and so the Spirit is free to guide us in our witnessing.

The forgotten element in witnessing is *listening*. Listening to God makes us sensitive to His Spirit's guidance. Listening to others helps us to understand their needs. We cannot help them until we understand them.

Many old people talk about themselves all the time. It is true that their active days may be over and their world seems to be narrowed down to their own personal affairs. Might you be one of these? Why center your world upon yourself? The greatest service of your life may be awaiting you. One of the greatest needs of the world today is for *listeners*. If you are incapacitated for any other service this ministry is still open to you. If you are willing to be an ear for the Lord, people will come to you. They want to be understood. They want to know about a Heavenly Father who can meet every need of every heart. This is witness indeed.

Chapter 17

When You Need
the Great Physician

Today as I write this chapter one of the boys in our church, fifteen-year-old Mike, was buried. He wanted to live, but he died of cancer. To the last his mother held faith that a miracle would happen. It didn't. My brother died of cancer just when it seemed a whole new ministry had opened up to him following his "retirement." The whole brotherhood prayed for his healing, but he was not healed. I know a number of others who *were* healed of cancer through prayer and God's special healing power. All I know to say is that "Why?" is not a question for me to ask of God.

I am also sure that the greatest prayer we can pray is, "Whatever brings the greatest glory to God I want, even if it means suffering and loss for me." One thing is sure, death *underscores* the witness of a good man sometimes beyond what might have been, had his life continued on earth.

No matter what happens we dare never be bitter or resentful. We must trust God to take everything and work it out to His glory. There are many things worse than death. Many people say this who have lost loved ones to an evil life or mental diseases.

The first purpose of our lives must be, "Thy

kingdom come, thy will be done." This is never a passive statement of endurance or of mere agreement to submit to whatever happens. It is a positive statement of the will to reach out for that which will bring glory to God.

To the true follower of Jesus, healing is not an isolated experience for special occasions or needs, it is an experience for the whole of life and for the whole person. Jesus' work of healing the body was only one part of his healing ministry. He healed people from sin and all its scars. He healed them from broken relationships. He healed them to be made whole persons with a new capacity to love.

A minister went through a terrible period of misunderstanding and unjust accusation. The unjustness created bitterness in his heart which led to soul sickness and despair and a sense of separation from God. One day he realized that he was yielding to a devastating type of death in his own soul. He prayed for forgiveness and for the ability to forgive the one who had wronged him, but he still felt helpless in his despair. After months of darkness he asked for anointing for healing as advised in James 5:13–16. The service was arranged and he was anointed for the healing of his spirit and his emotional life. He said, "After months of trying in my own strength and finding no relief, at the time of the anointing all the bitterness suddenly left me. God filled my heart with love for all, including the one who hurt me, and I was healed instantly." Then he added, "No one can tell me there is no God, not after His touch which came to me that day."

The greatest healing that can happen to anyone is the healing of the spirit.

A university professor's wife found herself consumed with fear and guilt when her beautiful daughter began to go out on dates. The memories returned which she thought long since buried of some things she herself had done in her teens. Although a leader in her church she did not think of turning to her pastor for help or to God for long-delayed forgiveness. She did the fashionable thing, she went to a psychiatrist. For a year the psychiatrist tried to get rid of her guilt complex. If it had been merely a complex he could have helped her, but this was plain guilt accentuated by present fears. It was only when she could no longer afford the psychiatrist that she turned to the Lord for forgiveness and healing of her spirit. When she did that and received healing, her "complex" was immediately gone. Forgiveness is always a healing miracle.

Sometimes people complain because they are not blessed by God as others have been. They do not realize that in thinking of themselves they open the door to bitterness and close it to God's grace. The big obstacle of God's grace is bitterness. "See to it that no one fail to obtain the grace of God; that no 'root of bitterness' spring up and cause trouble" (Hebrews 12:15). The Christian virtues of love, joy, peace, patience, kindness, goodness, faithfulness, gentleness, self-control are all healing virtues (Galatians 5:22). The opposite characteristics of enmity, strife, jealousy, anger, selfishness, envy make healing impossible (Galatians 5:20).

The negative emotions are sometimes called psychological poisons. They are poison and they lead to the all too prevalent psychosomatic diseases. Even if such condition starts "in the head" it does not stay there. It can become a real physical sickness. God wants to heal the whole person and the healing must start in our attitudes.

The question of suffering has always been a problem to the children of God. The early Christians suffered much. They were told: "Consider him who endured from sinners such hostility against himself, so that you may not grow weary or faint-hearted" (Hebrews 12:3). The Hebrew Christians were told that God would use their suffering for discipline to make them holy, which means *whole*.

God does not desire suffering as an end in itself, I am sure. But all suffering is so expensive He will not let it be wasted. He will use it for His children's growth.

Without question the person who has real faith has the best chance for health in the waning years, but bodies do wear out. It is hardly fair to expect God to give us at seventy-five or eighty vitality we had at twenty, but a Christian should have none of the ills that come from unchristian attitudes. Still, even in our weakness we must always be available for God's surprise miracles.

One of those surprise miracles happened in India in 1938. Lillian Grisso, a missionary, contracted encephalitis. Instead of sleeping all the time she could not sleep. As the disease advanced, making her helpless, the doctors pronounced her incurable and expected to return her to America as a permanent invalid.

I returned home from vacation in the hills in August and went over to our hospital to see Lillian. She told me the Lord had revealed to her that she was going to get well—in India. She wanted me to have faith in her, but I couldn't pick it up like that. Our doctor said to me, "Poor Lillian! She thinks she's going to get well. I believe in miracles, but not in this case."

I went away again to a conference. When I returned ten days later I saw a difference in Lillian, and while we prayed together God gave me the same faith for her healing. I did not try to have it, it was given to me. It became very easy to pray for her healing. A relapse of the disease came and the doctor said that was normal, but Lillian said she had to cooperate with God by having no fear, joy only. That was in September. By the next January she was back at her post in a girls' school. The Indians called her the "walking, walking miracle!"

That was thirty years ago. Lillian had several more terms of service in India and is now retired in a lively way in Indiana.

We are all His children, and He is the Great Physician who can heal even our anxieties.

I was surprised at the reaction of a wise friend to what I have written so far in this chapter. I thought I was talking about suffering all the time, but he says, "I cannot help feeling that you have somewhat slighted the whole problem of suffering. . . . You really say very little about it and your focus is on the miracle that happened to the Indian missionary. Miracles are miracles precisely because they are exceptional cases. Most people have simply to face up to 'all the ills the flesh is heir to.' "

All right, brother, I see that you are speaking for the majority of people who find it hard to think beyond their suffering. They do not realize that the Great Physician can make a difference in their suffering. I was thinking of one's attitudes that open the door for the Great Physician to do at least a measure of healing. But too many sufferers, I admit, resign themselves in glum apathy to whatever life has dealt them and do not even expect miracles— unless they are responsive to miracle drugs.

Nearly everyone is tempted to ask, "Why?" Some feel that they deserve suffering that comes to them, and others are sure they do not deserve what has happened to them. Perhaps the heart of the problem is in whether the deserving has anything to do with it or not. Is life set up on a merit system or not? Most people talk, at least casually, as if all were by merit.

This sounds good when life is gracious. A while ago I received an unmerited magnanimous gift of a trip for two to Europe for thirty days, all expenses paid. It was like a gift from heaven. It was like God's grace in that it was not mine until I took it. Many of my friends said, "You deserved it." Did I? If so, then what about when the reverse happens? Recently I came home sick from a weekend speaking engagement in a church, and added to my misery was the fact that my suitcase containing some irreplaceable things was stolen in the Washington, D.C., Union Station. If the merit system works in good fortune, it would also have to explain bad fortune.

The question of unmerited suffering was a real problem in Old Testament days. For Job in the midst of such suffering it was an agonizing problem. The people of that day thought that faithfulness to God brought deserved success and good fortune. God was just. So if bad fortune came it must be a man's fault because of some sin or shortcoming. Even today this problem is relevant as evidenced by the popularity of *J. B.* (Job) on Broadway.

There is drama in suffering and Job's experience was fast-moving drama, indeed. It was truly *More Than a Man Can Take,* as Wesley C. Baker titled it in his exciting study of Job.* Job was the man who had everything. Then in quick succession his servants were killed, his sheep and shepherds were destroyed by lightning, his camels were stolen, and all his children were killed by a cyclonic wind. "Then Job arose, and rent his robe, and shaved his head, and fell upon the ground, and *worshiped.* And he said, 'Naked I came from my mother's womb, and naked shall I return; the Lord gave, and the Lord has taken away; blessed be the name of the Lord' " (Job 1:20–21). This was not the end. Job became ill, his whole body was covered with loathsome sores. In his agony Job went out and sat on the ash heap. Then his wife came and taunted him for continuing his faith in God, but he had to hold onto that faith. It was all he had left. He had his faith

* W. C. Baker, *More Than a Man Can Take* (Philadelphia: Westminster Press, 1966).

before his suffering came and he would not give it up. Then three honorable men came as friends to comfort him. Seeing Job's agony they sat with him for seven days and nights without saying a word.

Finally Job could not take their gruesome silence any longer. He burst out with honest complaints for all this unmerited suffering. In acknowledging his suffering he was more able to face it, so that after hours of discussion on the philosophy of suffering from his friends Job could still cry out, "For I know that my redeemer lives" (Job 19:25).

Job did not know what we know today about a redeemer, but he knew enough to have hope and to hold onto that hope. He seemed to know that a relationship to God is the most important thing in life, that it is more important that God lives than that we live. Then verification came. God spoke to Job out of a whirlwind and all Job's questions became utterly irrelevant. God even asked Job questions and asked for dialogue. Job had contended that his suffering could not have come from hidden sin, but that no longer mattered. In the presence of God the grandeur of wonder restored Job to his true dignity. Job had wanted explanations but God gave him insights. Job came into an experience of humble dignity and integrity he had never known before:

> I had heard of thee by the hearing of the ear,
> but now my eye sees thee;
> therefore I despise myself,
> and repent in dust and ashes.

Job 42:5–6

To say "I believe" after such suffering is faith indeed. The restoration to Job of his health, wealth, family, and honor is really incidental to the story. So far I have neglected the prologue of this drama. Many Christians today who talk of the love of God say at the same time that disease, suffering, loss come from Him. They should read the prologue to Job. God *permitted* the tragedies to come, He did not bring them. Job was in His care all the time.

No matter what happens to us we are within His loving care. Our Lord suffered, Paul's thorn in the flesh was never taken away, we may suffer. If we trust Him, the suffering will never be useless. He is the Great Physician to the whole person. He always gives courage, hope, and faith.

Chapter 18

Death: Friend or Foe?

Does a child of God have reason to be afraid of death? It is true that many of us at times do have this fear, whether we have reason to or not Fears come from the unknown, but there is one thing we can know about the otherwise unknown future, that God is in it.

The apostle Paul had no fear of death because he knew Jesus as the risen Lord. We may enter into his faith: "So we do not lose heart. Though our outer nature is wasting away, our inner nature is being renewed every day. For this slight momentary affliction is preparing for us an eternal weight of glory beyond all comparison, because we look not to the things that are seen but to the things that are unseen; for the things that are seen are transient, but the things that are unseen are eternal" (2 Corinthians 4:16–18).

Thinking of death, I must tell you first about Miss Densie because she commissioned me with a message. Miss Densie was my Bible teacher when I was in my teens. After I left home I did not see her again for many years. By this time she lived in a retirement home where they called her "the angel of the home" because a visit with her was like a special visit from the Lord himself.

I last saw Miss Densie three weeks before she

died in great agony from cancer. I was told she might not know me, but as I entered her room she exclaimed, "Oh, Anna, I am so glad you have come. I wanted to tell you again to be sure to tell everyone that Jesus is alive, and I am going to Him very soon!" To her, death meant life everlasting.

My father never got old. At eighty-five the doctor told him he had a heart as strong as a man of twenty-five. A friend told me that he saw my father, at eighty-five, chin himself eighteen times! The longer he lived into his "retirement" years the more he traveled everywhere to preach. In his ninetieth year he averaged twelve sermons a month in all manner of out of the way places. He hunted out the little churches which no longer had a preacher, but he was also welcomed in many larger churches.

Father was never afraid of death. My sister, Mary, asked him when he was ninety if he did not fear death. He answered, "I have no fears. Statistics prove that more people die under ninety than over ninety."

He always said he wanted to die with his boots on—and he did. He was killed instantly by a drunken driver as he was being driven from one church to another fulfilling a preaching schedule. His funeral was *not* a sad occasion. People had too many warm, interesting stories to share about him as a teacher, preacher, and friend. There was nothing to be sad about because he wanted to serve until the last minute and then leave on schedule. He would have enjoyed his funeral. (Perhaps he did!)

Looking to a future life is not unique to Christianity. When I heard the Sound and Music program at the Pyramids near Cairo, Egypt, I was amazed again at the emphasis in ancient Egypt on the preparation for a future life. As soon as a man became a king, or pharaoh, he immediately began preparation for his life after death. This, of course, is the reason the pyramids were built. It explains all the fantastic array of priceless objects found in King Tut's tomb. One wonders what these kings did for their subjects when so much of their effort went into preparation for their own future.

A Christian prepares for his future in a different manner: he does it by *living* every day of his life in a way to be pleasing to God. His preparation is not in an accumulation of material treasures stored away, but in a life of love and service lived in this world now.

For the Christian who truly knows the Lord, the motivation for service is to please God and not merely to get a "reward" for himself in the future. As a child I heard about two churches on opposite corners of the street. In the one they sang, "Will there be any stars in my crown?" And the other church answered in singing, "No, not one." Perhaps that was their opinion of the neighboring church. In any case it always seemed off-color spiritually to sing: "Let me watch as a winner of souls; that bright stars might be mine in the glorious day." The problem seems to be that most Christians have been taught to believe that they should work for stars in their crowns. Then they unwittingly become stars in their own life drama and find themselves with inner conflict because of this religious self-centeredness.

The joy and peace of the Christian life come from commitment to Christ which frees one from self. We can have a taste of our future in Him right now, but it is only a taste. "For now we see in a mirror dimly, but then face to face. Now I know in part; then I shall understand fully, even as I have been fully understood" (1 Corinthians 13:12). The real reward is knowing God in Christ, and however dimly, the reward begins now.

In the early forties I was on a team for religious emphasis week in a midwestern college. The outstanding man on the team was Canon Bryan Green from the Church of England. Americans had a hard time pigeonholing Canon Green. Some thought he was too conservative and others thought him too liberal. Both types of leaders were on the team of twelve. The students enjoyed the variety and called for an open forum expecting a little excitement in such a confrontation. The excitement came when one of the students asked, "Mr. Green, do you believe in immortality?" Canon Green answered quickly and emphatically, "No!" Several of the leaders on the platform almost fell over, they were so shocked. Then Canon Green added, "I do not believe in immortality. That is a Greek idea. I believe in *eternal life* and that begins *now*."

Eteranl life does begin now. We have "today" and we live it in His presence and through strength given us by His Holy Spirit. So the shining secret is: If we are not afraid for *today* we need not be afraid for *tomorrow*.

How, then, *can* the fear of death possess anyone who knows the living Lord now? "So we are always of good courage; we know that while we are at home in the body we are away from the Lord, for we walk by faith, not by sight. We are of good courage, and we would rather be away from the body and at home with the Lord. So whether we are at home or away, we make it our aim to please him" (2 Corinthians 5:6–9).

For the man or woman who *knows* God, physical death is not even an interruption of the inner life. It is, rather, a great Setting Free.

Chapter 19

Can You Take "Useless" Years?

Greater than the fear of death for many persons is the fear of being helpless before death comes. I don't want to be an invalid myself. I don't want to be a burden to anyone. Neither do you.

I suppose the greatest security that comes to those who have bought living quarters in a retirement home is that there are arrangements available for their care if they do become invalided. This is especially true for those who are left alone in the world.

But even if one does become an invalid, as long as there is a mind that can think, no person needs to be useless.

Years ago I was on a City-wide Christian Mission in Duluth, Minnesota. As soon as I arrived people began asking if I had been to see Miss———. Finally I was taken to see this "hopeless" invalid. No one had spoken of her in a sad tone, only in an excited way. So I was really curious.

When I entered her room, there she was, completely paralyzed from her neck down—her hospital bed holding her in a sitting position. But she had a usable head that belonged to the Lord and she could pray. Her sister cared for her lovingly, and each morning after breakfast the sister brought out the prayer list. It was a roll of paper literally yards long, with hundreds of names on it. Each day that blessed woman went over the whole list, praying for each person as her sister held the paper before her.

People from far and near sent her requests for prayer. Every type of person, ministers included, came to her for new courage. She was known as the "power house of Duluth."

No one is ever useless who has a ministry of prayer. There are many people to perform the needed activities, but too few to take the time for prayer.

My mother had a fear of becoming an invalid but when it happened her faith in God carried her through. She spent her last seven years, not only helpless in body, but speechless, too, from several strokes. Her mind was clear though, her heart warm, one hand was still in good condition, and her listening ears were in perfect working order. She was in my home in Chicago for three years and she was a blessing to us all. Even some of my theological students would come to visit her and go away uplifted. She always smiled at the right time and her one hand could reach out and express the sympathy or joy of her heart.

I suppose the hardest thing about being "useless" is that it is much harder to receive help than to give it. It is much harder to be still than to be active. This is why it is important to learn how to be a gracious receiver as well as a gracious giver.

Some who are helpless are cared for in public or private institutions away from their families. But even here one need not "vegetate." The mind can be kept active in fellowship with God and any patient who always has a smile is a blessing to everyone who passes by. Every person known can be prayed for daily and so the hours will pass—creatively.

No one is ever useless to God but the problem in this busy world is that people are not very godlike. Urbanization and many other factors have broken up the family unit as a dynamic basic group in our society. And many people who have become helpless have had nothing in their lives to prepare them for creative adjustment to helplessness in a family or in an institution. They are simply not prepared for uselessness. Perhaps they demanded respect from their children even when they somehow knew they were unworthy of respect. Their children as they took on the responsibilities of adulthood forgot or did not care that their aging parents had growing needs. Of course, such older folk would feel uncared for and useless. It is hard for even mature adult children to feel a loving responsibility for immature old folk.

There is a Mexican legend about a man who did not want to be burdened any more with his feeble old father. He had his young son take the old man to a mountain cabin and leave him there with food and a blanket. The boy returned with half of the blanket. The father wanted to know why he brought half of the blanket back with him. The boy answered, "I am saving that for you, father."

I suppose the American equivalent of this legend is the old poem "Over the Hill to the Poorhouse." The picture of selfishness in that poem has had a devastating effect on our sentiments. Our modern beautiful homes for the aging are not even related to that old poorhouse, but the fear of sentimental criticism still lingers. One retired man of our acquaintance is opposed to any parents with children going to any institution. He says children owe it to their parents to care for them no matter what their need. To avoid criticism for their children other parents have made their own arrangements in case of helplessness and have so stated their desires in their wills.

The temptation to a feeling of uselessness will come even to those who have loved and have served in mature ways. Perhaps some of the parents who seemed so officious were merely fighting this fear of becoming useless. And the good ministers who loved their people with such abandon may not be escaping when they spend hours before the television, but may be fighting this fear, too. Paul Tillich said, ". . . people are sick not only because they have not received love but also because they are not allowed to give love, to waste themselves."* But surely such giving-love need never become a sickness. Perhaps the crux of the whole matter lies here: how to find meaning for living even though a person remains seemingly useless.

A retired woman, recently incapacitated for much service, told me she found great help from Dr. Frankl's logotherapy. I am not surprised. Dr. Viktor E. Frankl, professor of Psychiatry at the University of Vienna, had three horrible years at

* *The New Being* (New York: Charles Scribner's Sons, 1955), p. 48.

Auschwitz and other Nazi prisons. Partly because of the incredible suffering and degradation he suffered with others, he developed his theory that life must have meaning.* No matter how great a person's suffering or loss, he is still free to decide how he will take his condition, whether he will yield to it or stand up to it. In the process he will find that he becomes more concerned about a meaning for life than a meaning for suffering. In finding a meaning for life he can take whatever happens to him.

In adding a God-dimension to this experience, life has true meaning, even if there be nothing one can do for himself or for others. He can still worship. Worship makes thanksgiving possible. Thanksgiving opens the heart for God and for being a blessing to every available person. It will bring an end to any feeling of uselessness.

* See *Man's Search for Meaning* (Boston: Beacon Press, 1963).

Chapter 20

Have You Given Up Childish Ways?

My blind cousin Homer was in a nursing home because his wife was helpless from a stroke. All his life he had been a great reader but now he could not see. He loved to visit with people but the only other man in the nursing home was stone deaf. I came into Homer's room one day and found him slumped in a rocking chair—just sitting. When I called his name he jumped up, as alert as ever. Interest lit his face. As we visited he said, "I'm over ninety, I guess I'm in a *second childhood*." I said, "No, you aren't. No one needs to be in a second childhood. There is nothing wrong with old age but self-centeredness." He was silent a moment, and then he asked, "Is that really true?" I answered, "Yes." Then he said, "All right, I'll forget it! Come on and let me take you to see the fine new pastor who has just come to the church next door." He took me by the hand and led me lightheartedly down the street to the parsonage, his "second childhood" behind him.

How tragic that anyone should get the idea that he was *expected* to have a second childhood!

Recently I heard 1 Corinthians 13 read in a worship service. I had never paid too much attention to the last paragraph (vss. 8–13), but this day the words of that paragraph rang in my ears. You see, it was only a few weeks since I had visited Homer. In these lines, Paul wrote, "When I was a child, I spoke like a child, I thought like a child, I reasoned like a child; *when I became a man, I gave up childish ways*" (vs. 11). There is no room for a second childhood here. I wonder how many older people act childish because it is expected of them, or because they find it so easy to get away with it?

Eugenia Price has told me what Ma Sunday (Mrs. Billy Sunday) said a few years before her death: "I'm not a bit childish, really, but I've learned to act that way—it gives me more privacy when I want it and also more attention when I want it. Because I'm old—and look it—I get by with anything!" And Mrs. Sunday laughed.

It is expected of a three-year-old to be self-centered. He is just learning to know himself in relation to his little world. It is normal for him to be self-centered because he has just discovered himself. But if his parents are wise, he will find out that even though he is dearly loved, he is still not the center of the universe. He will learn to make room for others who are also important.

As a child learns to think of others he will grow out of doing things just to draw attention to himself. He will learn to have security within himself so he does not feel the need to lash out at others or to control them in order to feel that he is a human being with dignity. This is not the road to human dignity anyway.

A child is possessive of his toys as he learns the responsibility of ownership, but then he has to learn to share with others. The childish adult is possessive of people. A child is easily hurt; a childish adult is so touchy that he keeps account of wrongs people do "against him." One woman in a retirement home was giving me a tour of the place. When we entered the elevator an orderly got on with a cart, bound for the hospital floor. The woman said to me, "That's the way it is all the time. They always push me around and never let me be first." She kept her feelings extended, expecting others to step on them. Perhaps she wasn't in a second childhood, she just may never have grown out of her first!

God's picture of *true maturity* is in verses 4–7 in 1 Corinthians 13. "This love of which I speak is slow to lose patience—it looks for a way of being constructive. It is not possessive: it is neither anxious to impress nor does it cherish inflated ideas of its own importance. Love has good manners and does not pursue selfish advantage. It is not touchy. It does not keep account of evil or gloat over the wickedness of other people. On the contrary, it is glad with all good men when truth prevails" (Phillips). "Love does not insist on its own way; it is not irritable or resentful" (vs. 5, RSV).

The apostle Paul left no room for the Christian to revert to childish ways: "Love [which is maturity] knows no limit [even in years] to its endurance, no end to its trust, no fading of its hope; it can outlast anything" (Phillips).

Cousin Homer caught on. I hope you and I do, too. There is no room for a second childhood in the life of a child of God. We can keep on growing to the end of this life.

Chapter 21

Dying to Self at Sixty to Find the Best of Life

Recently a retired man, a church deacon, said he was tired of preachers talking about "dying to self." He is a good man and he thinks he knows his Bible. But his trouble is that he is thinking in Buddhist terms—not Christian. The Oriental idea of dying to self is to get rid of all self, all emotion, good as well as bad. The more "nothing" one becomes, the more godlike he is, for the Buddhist god is a great nothing.

The Christian idea of dying to self is entirely different. Out goes self-centeredness: "immorality, impurity, passion, slander [gossip], foul talk" (see Colossians 3:3–11). In comes the new nature: "compassion, kindness, lowliness, meekness, patience, love, peace, thankfulness" (see Colossians 3:-12–17).

What we must die to are the things in us that keep us from maturing: the characteristics which thwart joyous fulfillment of life. As we die to these "psychological poisons" we have a real chance for spiritual health and personal maturity.

Jesus knew what He was talking about when He said, "If any man would come after me, let him deny himself and take up his cross and follow me. For whoever would save his life will lose it, and whoever loses his life for my sake will find it" (Matthew 16:24–25). Jesus knew that this is the only way to the *abundant life* which He came to make possible for His followers (John 10:10).

Among Christians we are prone to talk about *sins* but the Bible talks about *sin*, which is turning against God and putting self first (Jeremiah 2:13 and all the teachings of Jesus). Even apart from the Bible, self-centeredness is child stuff, it is not maturity. Every time we put self first in any relationship we make a break in that relationship and automatically turn against God.

One woman said, "I am willing to put God first, but I am not willing to put my husband first." She did not realize that in putting God first her very inner nature would be changed so that she would automatically put her husband first.

In our relationship to others we are handicapped by the great American fear that someone will walk all over us. In this fear we miss the secret of Life: *Christ in you*. We are afraid to let self go for fear we will be trampled into nothing. But the truth of life and personal fulfillment is that a person never knows real dignity until he has stopped clinging to the wrong self, and has opened his life to the true self which is possible through Christ.

Why talk about this basic law of the Christian life to sixty-year-olds when they should have learned this at sixteen? The fact is that most Christians have not learned this basic lesson of life.

If this lesson has been poorly learned it may not show up very much while a Christian is active in service and is considered a very unselfish person for his busyness. The test comes when the activity stops! Does he now feel unwanted, unneeded, laid on the shelf, no good to anyone, unappreciated? All these feelings of being neglected are evidence of thinking from self-centeredness and they are all dangerous.

Any harsh judgment of others for their theological beliefs or manner of living or dressing is evidence that the gift of discernment and wisdom has been perverted into a selfish lashing out at others. This makes such people public nuisances because they cause divisions and stifle the growth of those still immature. The older a person becomes, the greater blessing he should be to all those who are still in places of active responsibility, the more encouraging he should be to those who are younger.

If you find yourself hardening in any of your attitudes it is time to take warning. Or perhaps you have let yourself go to the other extreme—complete indifference to others and to what is happening in the world. In any case, *it is never too late to begin all over again.* Perhaps you have never begun this kind of relationship with God and you feel you have no "abundant life" at all. For you it is also true: *it is never too late to begin.* Hope and a new beginning are always possible for anyone.

Have you stopped growing? Do you need to change? You can start today!

1. Commit or recommit your life to the Lord Jesus Christ. God is love and Jesus came to make that love plain to man. You need not be afraid of Him. He has abundant life waiting for you.

2. Accept His loving forgiveness for anything in

your past life which you do not like to remember. His forgiveness is real. He even "breaks the power of canceled sin." This means that even the *memory* of forgiven sin is cared for.

3. Look to the Lord Jesus Christ, a living Lord, for the gift of His Holy Spirit promised to every Christian, so that your new life is lived in His power.

4. God loves those around you and wants to draw them closer to Him. Even if some of them are ornery, still He wants them to know His love. You are His channel. See every person as Christ sees them and you will have His understanding. Don't waste the love of God—use it on these needy people.

5. When others correct you or criticize you, don't be touchy. Any hurt feelings you may have are evidence of some "old self" still hanging around. You want that old self to die. Let it die. Then look objectively at the criticism given. Perhaps it contains suggestions for your own growth. The criticism may also come out of the other person's own needs and he is, without knowing it, asking for your help. In either case thank God for light on the true situation.

6. Accept the prayer of Reinhold Niebuhr:

> God grant me serenity
> To accept the things I cannot change,
> Courage to change the things I can, and
> Wisdom to know the difference.

If we can learn to do whatever we can in any situation, and leave the unknown to God, we will find a new freedom from anxiety.

7. Guard against any *anxiety* about life, the future, family, friends, or the church. Anxiety is the enemy of faith and it is certainly its opposite. remember: "The Lord is at hand. Have no anxiety about anything, but in everything by prayer and supplication with thanksgiving let your requests be made known to God. And the peace of God, which passes all understanding, will keep your hearts and your minds in Christ Jesus" (Philippians 4:5–7).

8. Turn every concern into a prayer. God's concern is always greater than ours. You can cooperate with Him as you pray by helping Him to answer your prayers, even if it is no more than a smile or a show of loving patience.

9. Be thankful: for God and His love, for a redeemer, for the Holy Spirit. If you are suffering, thank God for doctors and nurses. If you are alone, be thankful that with Him you are never really alone.

10. Be available: to God for any service, to others for encouragement, to the Spirit of God for any manifestation of His love and power.

Dying to one's unreal, sinful, selfish self at sixty, seventy-five, or ninety can mean only the beginning of the real life in God which will never end. This is never a negative experience. There will be more consciousness of the new life in God than of death to the old self. The love of God works the miracle of a whole change in thought attitudes and life.

True faith is our willingness to *act* on what we have learned about the loving nature of God. We will not always feel young, but we can with sound minds choose our actions. I do not believe for one minute that we are only as old as we *feel*. Our bodies may wear out, our knees may stiffen, our joints may creak. But I do believe the Spirit-controlled child of God *is* only as old as he *thinks*.

Life is *life* at any age. So who's afraid of birthdays or of the passing years? If we are still learning, still growing, we can say to all who *are* afraid of the passing years:

> *Grow old along with me!*
> *The best is yet to be,*
> *The last of life, for which the first was made;.*
> *Our times are in His hand*
> *Who saith, "A whole I planned,*
> *Youth shows but half; Trust God, see all, nor be*
>   *afraid."*

Recommended Reading

Asquith, Glenn H. *Lively May I Walk,* Abingdon, 1960.

Devotions to help discover the wonderful treasure God has for you. (In large print.)

Baker, Wesley C. *More Than a Man Can Take,* Westminster, 1966.

A book on Job with insights into his suffering and cure.

Boas, Ernest P. (M.D.) and Norman F. (M.D.). *Add Life to Your Years,* John Day Co., 1963.

A.M.A. called it the best medical thinking on old age.

Bortz, Edward L., M.D. *Creative Aging,* Macmillan, 1963.

For courage and hope and wisdom born in living.

Cabot, Natalie Harris. *You Can't Count on Dying,* Houghton Mifflin, 1961.

Therefore use every opportunity for fulfillment.

Emmons, Helen B. *The Mature Heart,* Abingdon, 1953.

150 meditations, heartwarming and challenging.

Kaighn, Raymond P. *How to Retire and Like It,* Association Press, 1965. A small book with everything in it you wonder about.

Koch, Roy S. *Zestful Living for Older Adults,* Herald Press, 1963.

A small pamphlet. Advice on living long without aging.

Peck, Joseph H., M.D. *Let's Rejoin the Human Race,* Prentice-Hall, 1963.

A verbal spanking of American myths about later life.

President's Council on Aging. *On Growing Older.* Helpful advice and warnings against fads. For this and other government bulletins write:
Director, Public Information Staff
Administration on Aging (AOA)
330 Independence Ave., S.W.
Washington, D.C. 20201

Price, Eugenia. *The Beloved Invader,* Lippincott, 1965.
A novel about real people who faced joy, sorrow, and loss in a most Christian manner.

The Retirement Council (One Atlantic Street, Stamford, Conn. 06901). *101 Ways to Enjoy Your Leisure.*
Excellent on all kinds of crafts and other interests.

Taylor, Florence M. *The Autumn Years,* Seabury Press, 1968.
Insights and reflections relevant to almost any situation you will meet.

Whitman, Virginia. *Around the Corner from Sixty,* Moody Press, 1967.
The last years can be a crescendo in fulfillment. Many illustrations for encouragement.

You may like to join the American Association of Retired Persons, which includes a bimonthly magazine, *Modern Maturity.* The magazine keeps you in touch with thrilling people and adventures. Write:
AARP Membership Division
406 East Grand Ave.
Ojai, California 93023.